T0122166

Glow and Grow in the Grace of God

Ann Lynn Noble and Carlisle Hope Noble

WestBow
PRESS®
A DIVISION OF THOMAS NELSON
& ZONDERVAN

Scripture taken from the New Life Version (NLV) Copyright
© 1969 by Christian Literature International
Scripture quotations marked (NIV) are taken from the Holy Bible, New
International Version®, NIV®. Copyright © 1973, 1978, 1984, 2011 by Biblica,
Inc.™ Used by permission of Zondervan. All rights reserved worldwide. www.
zondervan.com The "NIV" and "New International Version" are trademarks
registered in the United States Patent and Trademark Office by Biblica, Inc.™
Scripture taken from the King James Version of the Bible.

WestBow Press books may be ordered through booksellers or by contacting:

WestBow Press
A Division of Thomas Nelson & Zondervan
1663 Liberty Drive
Bloomington, IN 47403
www.westbowpress.com
1 (866) 928-1240

ISBN: 978-1-9736-2572-8 (sc)
ISBN: 978-1-9736-2571-1 (hc)
ISBN: 978-1-9736-2573-5 (e)

Library of Congress Control Number: 2018904376

Print information available on the last page.

WestBow Press rev. date: 05/15/2018

Glow and Grow in the Grace of God
by
Best-selling author Ann Lynn Noble
Emerging author Carlisle Hope Noble
With comments by Kendall Noble and Caitlin Noble

Don't push children aside as if they don't matter, as the
disciples tried to do. Jesus said, "Let the little children
come to Me. Do not stop them. The holy nation of heaven
is made up of ones like these." (Matthew 19:14 NLV)

Are you aware—as so many are—that God is powerfully gifting
children, and that He is using these children to talk to the world?
Are you aware that these gifted children are becoming accustomed
to walking easily with their Lord in a supernatural normal?
God speaks to us through the scriptures, through other people,
and through the Holy Spirit. It was under the Holy Spirit's leading
that this book was possible for me to write. Much prayer has gone
into having any thoughts as to what was to be written under each
chapter title. The titles were the first things I wrote down, and as I
approached each one in prayers, the thoughts would finally flow.
As I was writing, my excitement about this
book and childlike faith grew.

Contents

Preface by the Coauthor

Read this. It will change your life for real.

Hi, this is Carlisle Hope Noble speaking. (I'm twelve and in the seventh grade.) Now, if you are reading this it probably means that you're bored and have nothing else to read. Or you are the type of person who reads the introduction and the About the Author section plus all the reviews. Both of those types of people are perfectly fine. What I want to get through to you is that this book is incredible, and all the stories in here to me are true miracles. The main thing I want you to know is that this is truly an inspired book.

When you think of a book inspired by the Holy Spirit, you probably think that when you read these pages they are going to be spectacular and stupendous—something worthy of God's talents. Even when I, the coauthor, started reading this book, I thought it was okay, but it wasn't God-worthy. As I started to read deeper, the whole book just got stranger to me. This is because the way the book is written is so different from the way the world talks today. Example: if you were saying to people, "This morning the still small voice inside me said we need to start walking in the supernatural normal today, your natural and my super," people would stare at you, thinking you were some weirdo. This whole book talks in this way and isn't afraid of what the world will say.

The way it is written is foreign to the world but must be normal and beautiful to God. Even as a strong Christian I, like most of you, have grown into the world where the way this book talks is strange to us. One night in my bed, I was reading the thirty-one-day devotional of *Restore, Restore, Restore and More*. That night I came to this powerful conclusion: this could be how God talks all the time, and this is truly God's inspired book. Through the Holy Spirit, He inspired us to write it. I felt the presence of the Holy Spirit, and I couldn't help but start crying because I knew that I—a random child—was looking at a manuscript of a God-inspired book and that I was a part of it.

Endorsements

"I have known Ann Noble for more than six years, and in each book she writes, she shares her faith and love for God and encourages her readers to grow in their relationship with Christ, and this book *Glow and Grow* is no different. In *Glow and Grow,* Ann shares the powerful message of becoming who we are in Christ and growing in our walk with the Lord. Ann Noble is a dear friend and a precious woman of God who shares inspirational stories and the wisdom of God in each book she authors. I highly recommend this book and know that your life will be transformed as you read it."

—Michele Grace Pillay, evangelist,
World Voice of Hope Foundation

"What a totally unique concept: grandmother and granddaughter coauthoring a book. And what a blessing their relationship proves to be. Terrific insight from the wisdom of years to the awakening of youthful faith. A delightful read."

—Laurie Magers, executive assistant
to Zig and Tom Ziglar, Ziglar, Inc.

"It's time to hear from children! Adults, it is time we did our part to make that possible. For several years, prophets have been declaring that the next major move of God will occur with young people leading the way. Ann and her granddaughter, Carlisle (aided occasionally by younger sisters Kendall and Caitlin), meet today's prophecies head on in a book that spans the generations with God's practical and loving wisdom. With grandmother and granddaughter each giving their perspectives, *Glow and Grow in the Grace of God* begins with an in-depth look at the protection promises of Psalm 91. This essential book ushers parents, grandparents, children, and Christian mentors into the practical knowledge and skills needed to assist Christian youth in fulfilling their vital callings, not some day, but now."

—Marjorie Russell Kough, editor, author,
CEO Testimony Publications

"Ann Noble has the heart, the passion, and the expertise you need to listen to. This book is a beautiful and necessary story of faith, love, and living out what we are called to. Every generation will love it."

—Gabrielle Jackson Bosché, best-selling author
and Millennial expert

"I've known Ann since elementary school. It's been all these years, and I never knew she was such a gifted writer. Every book is more fun to read than the last. And I'm not saying the first one wasn't. It was thrilling, exciting, astonishing, and challenging.

Her gift for remembering and detailing pertinent events in her life to illustrate her points just amazes me. She makes the whole thing come alive with these little stories, and I'm always eager for the next one.

And the great thing is, Carli has inherited that storytelling gift.

This is an awesome book.

I am blown away by Carli's level of maturity that shows in her writing, that she prays so naturally, as well as discerningly, and that she has the strength of faith that she does. A real woman of God, even in grade school. Breathtaking."

—Mrs. Sarah Kuhn Welte, Oklahoma City, Oklahoma

"My dear friend and cohost in the Global Intercession Team Healing Ministry has just written a new book in a voice full of wisdom and wit. I want to add this is a winsome voice that draws a reader in to the essence of what it takes to raise up children in the way they should go, the goal of every loving parent. I felt myself glowing and growing as she related true stories and explanations in her simple, clear way.

To add the voices of her three granddaughters, including guest author Carlisle, was a gift from God. Carli is a mature-voiced preteen who is highly gifted with maturity and style. I look forward to hearing more from these two wonderful authors, though Carlisle is now only twelve. What a hit. Don't miss this treasure house, a glimpse of Kingdom practices that work through trial, storm, and calm, to raise a family that glows and grows. I am honored to give a glowing endorsement of *Glow and Grow in the Grace of God*."

—Anne Swartout, Ridgefield, Connecticut

"Ann Noble and her granddaughter Carlisle have created a gem with their book *Glow and Grow in the Grace of God*. From the first word on, it is evident that Ann and Carlisle have listened intently for the Lord's direction concerning the message they are meant to convey. How refreshing and original to hear the Word expressed through the vantage point of both adult and child, each offering its own unique insight. I recommend this book highly and trust that its stories and rich messages will transform readers."

—Jena Lamse, director of guidance counseling,
Legacy Christian Academy

Acknowledgments

I first thank You, dear heavenly Father, for allowing me to experience—so many years ago—a prophetic voice of a child. The results of that so enriched my life. That was over thirty years ago, and I have never forgotten it.

Next, I thank You, Holy Spirit, for the vision and purpose of this book, complete with guidance in writing. I would have no idea what to write, but suddenly it was clear in my mind, and the writing would flow. That happened each time I got to a new spot. You were always there. Indeed, I thank You, Holy Spirit.

I thank you, sweet Carlisle, for wanting to write with me and for your hours in prayer as we were being led as to what to write. I thank God for her giftings, wisdom, and alacrity in this project.

I thank my family for patiently letting Carlisle and me push through to get this done, even when things seemed not to be moving. This book had to be God's insight, not ours. God knows the plan He has for each and every one of us, the gifts that are needed, and all that goes into our walking in that path. Carlisle and I couldn't set out on our own and write this.

I thank God for ideas for the chapter titles and moving us through His thoughts for each one. What an experience.

I thank Marjorie Russell Kough for editing this book, pushing through situations at her end to get it done. It is a delight to work with you, Marj, and I admire your ability to get inside a book, the author's voice, and the reader's needs.

I thank you, Steve Kasyanenko and Gabrielle and Brian Bosche for that conference you held in 2016 that gave a voice to that first book, *Restore, Restore, Restore and More*. Without your mentoring, your encouragement, and your friendship, these three books written since would still be in my head.

I thank Nancy Knapp Wilkinson, my friend since age twelve and later becoming my sister-in-law, for wanting to design the cover of this book. Her talent is a gift from God, and it is amazing. Thank you so very much, Nancy. Thank you for your cheerleading from the start.

Thanks to all my endorsers, my first readers of this book. Your words were a confirmation we really did hear from God. Laurie, the help you gave me, after decades of helping Zig Ziglar turn out book after book, is measureless.

Thank you, Bob, for your steadfast love over the fifty-two years of our marriage. May we have many, many more.

Introduction

Recently on a radio interview, when asked how I came to write this book, I replied that I really couldn't explain it—there was just a "knowing" in my spirit that it is what God wanted me to do. It was as if I knew I had to stop what I was working on and write a book for parents and children, pointing out children's strong giftings from the Lord. Children are so receptive to learn from Him. I have been aware for some time now that God is using children more and more. The Bible speaks of it, and I'll give you examples of that in chapter 1. I've experienced it. That story is shared in this book as well.

Children's voices are to be heard. God is using them as He always has. We just haven't been paying close enough attention.

Don't push children aside as if they don't matter, as the disciples tried to do. Jesus said, "Let the little children come to Me. Do not stop them. The holy nation of heaven is made up of ones like these" (Matthew 19:14 NLV).

We are told not to push children away. What better reason than that for me to ask our granddaughter, Carlisle, to coauthor this book? She just turned twelve a few days ago, but when we started this book, she was eleven. When I asked her if she would like to write this book with me, she asked if her little sisters—Kendall, age eight at that time, and Caitlin, age six—could help. Absolutely. I knew they were aware of God moving in their lives, so certainly we could use their help. Their input helps all of us see God through children's eyes at three different ages.

I'm delighted to write this book, and as with my first book, *Restore, Restore, Restore and More,* I can't wait to see what it says. At this point, I have no idea.

I do know about God's leading and insight, so I know this will be a great blessing for families as they watch their children start to glow and grow in the Lord.

A typo of mine and creative thinking by my sister-in-law and cover artist, Nancy Wilkinson, created this title, *Glow and Grow in the Grace of God.* I was intending to type "Grow in the Grace of God," but when I saw the word *Glow* written instead, I really liked it. Nancy did too. She combined them both, and it perfectly describes what God does with all of His children. So the title officially became *Glow and Grow in the Grace of God.*

As Carlisle and I approached each chapter title, we sought direction through prayer as to what He wanted those chapters to reveal. We eagerly sought that direction, for how else could this book be written? Carlisle and I both humbly realize that it is an amazing honor to be able to send out this important message.

 Carlisle is very artistically talented. This anime picture was an art assignment at her school. When Bob and I attended Grandparents' Day for the sixth graders and saw this hanging on the wall, immediately I knew the image would be perfect for this book. It will let you know when Carlisle is writing.

"Truly I tell you, anyone who will not receive the kingdom of God like a little child will never enter it" (Luke 18:17 NIV).

Let's see what receiving the Kingdom of God looks like to a child.

Dedicated to

Our son Tom and our daughter-in-law Jessica, who blessed us with three beautiful granddaughters: Carlisle, Kendall, and Caitlin.

Chapter 1

Just Use Your Childlike Faith

It was a lovely day in Chicago. Bob and I had gone downtown to meet our son, Tom, for lunch. He had flown in from Texas on business. Lunch was over, and Tom needed to go back to work. Bob and I were waiting for the valet to bring our car to the front of the hotel. I happened to glance around toward the door of the Palmer Hilton just as a nicely dressed young woman wheeled a man, who I assumed was her husband, through the door in a wheelchair. The man had lost both of his legs at the knee.

A Vision from God

As if actually happening before my eyes, I had a vision of his legs growing back. Both of his legs, which were beneath blue pants that had been hemmed to reach around the knee joints, just started stretching out. The missing length of his legs appeared, and then his feet. The vision was unfolding fast, and the man seemed to be watching as I was, in sincere amazement. It didn't seem that it caused him any pain. His wife didn't appear aware of what was happening. She was carefully maneuvering the wheelchair through the crowd of people walking up and down past the hotel.

Our car pulled up immediately after that, and I got in on the passenger side. As Bob slid into the driver's seat, all I could say was, "That was amazing."

"What was amazing?" Bob asked.

I told him what I had just seen in that vision. Neither of us said much after that. I think I was in shock and awe, and Bob was trying to absorb my words.

That was my first and only experience with an open vision, but the Bible lets us know they are real. There are eleven visions mentioned in the Bible, and the prophet Joel spoke of it happening in the last days in Joel 2:26–27. We all have had dreams, but a vision while I was awake? That was a new thing. Let's look at what Acts said that Joel spoke of regarding visions.

These people are not drunk, as you suppose. It was only nine in the morning!

No, this is what was spoken by the prophet Joel:

"In the last days, God says,
'I will pour out my Spirit on all people.
Your sons and daughters will prophesy,
your young men will see visions,
your old men will dream dreams.
Even on my servants, both men and women,
I will pour out my Spirit in those days,
and they will prophesy.
I will show wonders in the heavens above
and signs on the earth below,
blood and fire and billows of smoke.
The sun will be turned to darkness
and the moon to blood
before the coming of the great and glorious day of the Lord.
And everyone who calls
on the name of the Lord will be saved'" (Acts 2:15–21 NIV).

I didn't expect a vision, and I don't think we should expect it to be an ordinary occurrence. God can do anything He wants to do to speak to us. The Bible tells us everything we need to know. Showing me that vision really got my attention, and I remember it as if it happened today.

I thought about that for several days. Finally, I talked to God about it. This is exactly what I said to Him: "Lord, I am thrilled that You are going to create new limbs for those who have lost or never had them, for You know how thankful I have been most all of my life for my arms, legs, feet, and hands. I've always been thanking You for them. I just really don't think I am the one to work through. I don't have that much faith."

Just Use Your Childlike Faith

Immediately—and I mean immediately—I knew. Somehow, I just knew I was only to use my childlike faith. And just as quickly as I understood that, I understood and said, "Oh! It will just happen. It will be fine." And that settled it.

So what exactly happened in the several days that I thought about that vision and finally told God that I just wasn't the one, that I just didn't have that much faith?

What I believe happened is that my adult faith (that's what I'll call it) factored in all the impossibilities that I could think of, totally forgetting that with God, all things are possible. However, when I understood to just use my childlike faith, all that thinking I was doing about me, my limitations, and the impossible medical restrictions—everything impossible about it was instantly gone.

God Speaks to Us

Let's consider 1 Samuel 3:8–9 (NIV):

"A third time the LORD called, 'Samuel!' And Samuel got up and went to Eli and said, 'Here I am; you called me.'

"Then Eli realized that the LORD was calling the boy. So Eli told Samuel, 'Go and lie down, and if he calls you, say, 'Speak, LORD, for your servant is listening.' So Samuel went and lay down in his place."

Samuel is the son of Hannah. Hannah was happily married but couldn't conceive a child. She went to the temple and poured out her heart to God in prayer. Hannah even promised God that if He would give her a son, she would give him to the Lord for his ministry.

God did answer her prayer. Samuel is that son, and as promised, she gave him to Eli the priest to train him for the ministry—probably between the ages of three and four. Hannah had more children, the Bible tells us, but it lets us know that each year Hannah made a new priestly robe for her growing boy and took it to him (1 Samuel 2:19).

One night while Samuel was sleeping, he heard his name called. Sure that it was Eli calling, Samuel went into Eli's room, asking what he needed. Eli told him that he hadn't called him, and Eli told Samuel to go back to bed. Samuel did go back to bed, but a second time he heard his name called. Once again he went into Eli's room, and once again Eli sent him back to bed. It happened again. A third time Samuel heard his name, and a third time went to Eli. This time, Eli realized that the Lord was calling for the boy (v. 9). He told Samuel to lie down again and if he heard his name a fourth time, to say, "Speak Lord, for your servant is listening."

When God calls your name four times, He really wants to speak to you. It took a while for Eli to realize what was going on, but when he did, he taught the little boy how to hear from the Lord. God needed Samuel to take an important message to Eli.

Are we parents or grandparents teaching our children that God still speaks today? Perhaps Eli had not done so before that night, since he thought Samuel was too young. God knows everything. God knew Samuel was ready, and He had quite a long, harsh message for the little boy to deliver to Eli.

Samuel heard his name that fourth time, and he said, "Speak

Lord, for your servant is listening." God then spoke to Samuel. Let's listen in:

"The LORD came and stood there, calling as at the other times, 'Samuel! Samuel!'

"Then Samuel said, 'Speak, for your servant is listening.'

"And the LORD said to Samuel: 'See, I am about to do something in Israel that will make the ears of everyone who hears about it tingle. At that time I will carry out against Eli everything I spoke against his family—from beginning to end. For I told him that I would judge his family forever because of the sin he knew about; his sons blasphemed God, and he failed to restrain them'" (1 Samuel 3:10–13 NIV).

God had already spoken to Eli about this. Eli's own sons were rebels. It said they blasphemed God. In other words, they spoke irreverently about God and His ways. God told Eli to discipline them, but he never did successfully. Therefore, God went through the little boy under Eli's roof to deliver the message, the warning, once again.

"Jesus Christ is the same yesterday and today and forever" (Hebrews 13:8 NIV).

This makes me think. Has God been trying to tell me something that I haven't done? Has God sent a child to deliver a message to me? I guess we had better be alert, for the Lord is the same yesterday, today, and forever.

Why Does God Require Faith?

The Bible tells us our faith is enormously important to God. Why is this so? Ephesians 2:8 is a huge reason:

"For it is by grace you have been saved, through faith—and this is not from yourselves, it is the gift of God—not by works, so that no one can boast" (Ephesians 2:8–9 NIV).

To be saved means that by believing that Jesus died for our sins on the cross, we are rescued from God's judgment and the punishment of eternal separation from Him. And that is through faith.

"And without faith it is impossible to please God, because anyone who comes to him must believe that he exists and that he rewards those who earnestly seek him" (Hebrews 11:6 NIV).

God loves it when we seek Him, and He loves when we want to have a strong relationship with Him and enjoy being around Him. Like any other relationship, one with God requires our time together, trust, respect, and love. We do trust and have faith in God and in His love for us. Because God loves us so much, He provides for our needs in many different ways, which will be addressed through the chapters of this book.

He needs us to think about this. Maybe you think your faith is weak, but you probably have stronger faith than you realize you do. God needs us to realize the difference between childlike faith and our adult faith. We must know what we need to avoid.

This first chapter is called "Childlike Faith," so I asked Carlisle what that meant to her, and I also asked her to interview her little sisters to see what their thoughts were. Carli did interview them, and she did an amazing job—even asking well thought-out questions about their faith, which allowed them to understand her main question: What is childlike faith? What does childlike faith look like to an eleven-, eight-, and six-year-old? I will let Carli explain her thoughts and also report our other two granddaughters' answers to the same question.

What Is Childlike Faith?

Childlike faith is when you wholeheartedly believe God can do anything. See, a child will believe you because their minds are still pure and untouched by the reality of the world that all humans grow into. We, as Christians, aren't to grow into the world's reality. We are supposed to change for the better, realizing there is a supernatural way God does things.

If you told children there was a unicorn outside, they would run to the window and say, "Where?" They wouldn't have a single doubt. That is how we are supposed to trust God. Adults have jobs and sometimes families to support, making less and less time for God, forcing them to rely more on themselves. I spend time with God without these distractions. But even at eleven or almost twelve now, I'm starting to lose that kind of faith. That is why you must stay in true prayer with God.

Carli's insight is amazing. She just turned twelve a few weeks ago, but already she's figured out one of the big problems God has with adults. We give Him less and less time, therefore leaning on our own understanding, which can't deal with impossible things.

Carli has a keen understanding of true prayer, and she will be explaining that in another chapter. Meanwhile, she explains what Kendall and Caitlin said when she asked them to explain childlike faith.

Kendall is eight and said that kids are less uptight about their faith, but adults are "by the book" and have to think things over and question God, questions like who He is and why He does this and that.

Caitlin came into the room, and I asked her what childlike faith was as a six-year-old. She had to think about it a little while. Then she answered this way: "It is when you are just starting your walk with Christ and are very curious about your faith. You think God is invincible."

I looked at the paper, read what Carlisle had written, and asked, "Did Caitlin really use the word *invincible*?"

"Yes," Carli said.

I asked, "Where did she learn such a big word?"

"Probably from the movies," Carlisle answered.

That makes sense. What a great way to describe God.

Okay, let's think about this: for three days, when I thought and thought about God having me pray for limbs to be restored, I did exactly what Kendall said adults do. My answer, having thought it through, was, "Nope, I am not the one with that much faith." I totally felt that that open vision indeed was from God, but no way could I see limbs growing back happening as I prayed.

Who was I looking at?

What was I focusing on?

Me.

And I was right. I couldn't, as hard as I wished, make limbs be restored.

The Holy Spirit showed me to just use my childlike faith, and that settled it.

My thoughts immediately switched to God. It will be the powerful supernatural Holy Spirit at work, and it will just happen. It will be fine. I will pray with the faith of these children.

Let's look again at what a child says that the faith they use looks like. Carlisle said that she wholeheartedly believes God can do anything. Remember, she pointed out that her life is not full of the distractions of a job or a family. "I spend time with God without those distractions," she said.

This is true. Her relationship with God is pure love without a motive, without worries—just Carlisle and God, spending time together.

For a younger view, eight-year-old Kendall pointed out that kids aren't uptight about what God says. They don't have to think about it or ask questions about it.

That is certainly what I had done. I thought hard and long for three days before I talked to God about it. I knew all that healing would involve, and I came up with only one answer: "No, I just don't have that much faith."

If God had asked eight-year-old Kendall to pray for limbs to grow out, this thinking about it would not have occurred. Kendall would have accepted as fact that God is restoring limbs. It will happen, she would think, because God said so.

Caitlin said, "I am just starting my walk with Christ, and this is what I have learned: God is invincible."

What an impressive word for that age, but I had forgotten that she saw an animated movie with that word in the title. It was full of invincible characters, each with a special gift that made the family do amazing things.

God is invincible, incapable of being defeated or conquered. Definitely, God is a superhero. He is invincible.

Childlike, Not Childish

I want to stop right here and make sure that we are not confusing childlike faith with childish faith. Childish faith is often applied contemptuously; in other words, with disrespect. This childish faith is unsuitable for a grownup or anyone else. Childlike faith is what pleases our heavenly Father.

Let's try to stay in our childlike faith. Let's try to live our whole life in this faith. The results will be staggering, as we are not putting brakes on God, not limiting Him by thinking things through as an adult.

An Eight-Year-Old Child Becomes King

In 2 Kings 2:22, we learn about King Josiah, the last king of Israel. I bring him up because he was only eight years old when he became king. Josiah reigned thirty-one years and is known for instituting major religious changes. You see, he sought God, which is amazing considering who Josiah's father and grandfather were. His grandfather was King Manasseh, and his dad was King Amon. Both were very wicked kings.

King Manasseh was actually known as the worst of the worst of kings, as far as leading a country away from God. He was twelve when he became king, just a boy himself. He introduced the foreign ways of worshipping, practices such as manmade idols to worship, sacrificing children, and consulting mediums and wizardry. He even sacrificed one of his own sons.

When Manasseh died, his son Amon became king. Amon was twenty-two when he took over, but he picked up right where his dad left off—just as evil.

King Amon's servants conspired against him and killed him in his own home, so Amon only reigned two years.

That left eight-year-old Josiah to lead the country. God can use a child to influence a nation, and thankfully, this little boy had a heart after God. I can only assume that someone, perhaps his grandmother or mother, taught Josiah about God and King David. I was curious, so I did some searching. I found that his mother was Jedidah. She was married to that man who did everything against God, but I learned she quietly sought God and raised her son to honor Him, evidently seeking wise council while she helped her little eight-year-old rule as king. We know older people helped King Josiah at first, but when he was fifteen, he started to seek the Lord on his own. He followed good examples, like David.

Josiah ordered the temple to be rebuilt, and during that time, the workers found a scroll hidden in the walls. They took it to Josiah to read, and as he read, this young boy was very alarmed to learn that he and all the people of Israel had been sinning.

They had been worshipping false gods. This worship of false gods was the way with so many of the people, since that is what King Manasseh and King Amon encouraged. Josiah was very brave in ordering the false gods that people had built to worship knocked down. He broke up those idols and got rid of them.

The scroll had been lost for so many years that the people had lost sight of what God asked them to do. Josiah was so sad, so angry, that he tore his clothes. That was what they did in those days to show grief and repentance. Then he set in motion a reformation to destroy those idols. That reformation bears his name and left an indelible mark on Israel's religious traditions. The faith of a young king who loved the Lord moved that mountain. (You can read about Josiah in 2 Kings 22–23:30.)

I turned seventy-five years old less than a week before Carli turned eleven. God knows Carlisle, Kendall, and Caitlin walk in childlike faith. Childlike faith is such a pure faith, and we adults can use it too. In less than a blink of an eye, I reverted back into that pure, simple trust when led to use that childlike faith regarding limbs growing back. This is how powerful childlike faith is. You can hop back into it in a split-second. Let's stay there. Let's stay in that childlike, mountain-moving faith.

Chapter 2

Psalm 91: I've Got It Made in the Shade of God's Shadow

I love Psalm 91 and the power it punches. I pray it over situations that arise. But I was a little surprised that God seemed to want a child to study this chapter; I was, that is, until I took a look, verse by verse, through all sixteen verses.

This chapter is perfect for children to study, to memorize, to store in their hearts. Fears are not uncommon, but I totally felt this chapter was to be included. Indeed, it does take control of every fearful situation: every single one of them. I have looked at each one as an adult. I told Carlisle that I would do the adult view, and I wanted her to look over Psalm 91 verse by verse with Kendall and Caitlin. Then we would weave the different views together. They have already started memorizing these verses, and I will as well.

Psalm 91 tells how God protects us. We just have to do our part. We will see what our part is, and as we study this, we'll see just how important it is that we do our part. What I really like is that Carlisle has some excellent examples of personally experiencing this protective power of God.

We want to go over this psalm with you verse by verse. I will write the verses out, but I would like for you to open your Bible, because it may be a different translation. The verses we use here are all from the New International Version (NIV) of the Bible. Comparing translations will give further insight. I underline and make notes in my Bible. You may want to do that with some of the things we learn.

"Whoever dwells in the shelter of the Most High will rest in the shadow of the Almighty" (Psalm 91:1).

God is our shelter when we are afraid. God is my protector and will carry me through dangers and fears of life. What better time than at the ages these three girls are—six, eight, and eleven—to take this chapter and hide it in their heart. We are set on memorizing all sixteen verses. Also, we challenge you to memorize Psalm 91 along with us.

I like how this verse tells us we'll be in the shadow of the All-Powerful. See, when there is a shadow over you, someone is standing right by you. So, if you are in God's shadow, it means He is standing right there with you, protecting you. I really like that.

"I will say of the Lord, 'He is my refuge and my fortress, my God, in Whom I trust'" (Psalm 91:2).

He is my protector and will carry me through all the dangers and fears I face in my life. We are to say that to God each morning and each night, as well. Say, "You are my safe and strong place, heavenly Father, and I am trusting You to protect me."

When all else fails, and your parents aren't there to talk to, God is still always there to protect and guide you thankfully. We can for sure trust our parents, and we can for sure trust God.

"Surely he will save you from the fowler's snare and from the deadly pestilence" (Psalm 91:3).

This should be a verse we carry through our lives. We should simply trust ourselves to God's protection. Deadly diseases may be around us, but they can't touch us as we hide in the shadow of our Almighty God. Satan may place traps, but they are rendered useless as God unarms them or changes our paths.

Give God the Credit

Remember, God is the one who protected you and healed you. Give God the credit and thank Him. You don't have to feel you are alone to face these things. God is right there.

That's good, Carlisle. Give God the credit for protection, for healing. We need to give God the credit due Him and not just take all this for granted. Thank you for pointing that out. Let's remember to say thank You to our heavenly Father for all He does that has been going unnoticed and seemingly unappreciated by us.

"He will cover you with his feathers, and under his wings you will find refuge; his faithfulness will be your shield and rampart" (Psalm 91:4).

We can picture ourselves hiding safely under His wings, or riding inside the strong walls of an armored truck created by God to protect us. Carry those pictures with you, for both of those are descriptions from the Word.

That verse is very clear. When I see an armored truck, I'll remember that when I see armored trucks at grocery stores to pick up money and other places.

"You will not fear the terror of night, nor the arrow that flies by day" (Psalm 91:5).

The Bible warns us that the night is the enemy's playground, and we should be safely asleep at home. As I wrote this on June 12, 2016, the news was filled with information about the senseless killings in an Orlando, Florida, nightclub, killings that took place at 2 a.m. Evil lurks in some men, wanting only to harm, but in God's shadow, where we rest if we choose, we will not be afraid. Know that He is protecting those of us resting in His shadow. Trust our heavenly Father as a child clings to his or her daddy. Trust His protection.

There are challenges day and night. You can't get away from them, but you can trust God to protect you. And we can use common sense and stay safely at home when it is late at night.

The arrow that flies in the day reminded me of when our neighborhood suddenly looked like *The Wizard of Oz,* with shingles whirling around that had blown off roofs. It wasn't a tornado, but straight-line winds that destroyed roofs and knocked over fences all over our neighborhood—but our house was just fine.

I Prayed Psalm 91

My practice has been to pray Psalm 91 over our house, and indeed, it was as if the hand of God had been cupped over our home and our neighbors' homes on either side. I knew that was not just coincidence. I knew that God had protected us. Most of the roofs have now been repaired, and there are new fences all over the place, but there are still a few homes with blue tarps covering holes as homeowners wait their turn to get a new roof. I thank God so very much that ours was untouched.

One of my neighbors was at her computer when that front came through. She said she could hear the nails being sucked out of the wood in her fence. I went over to see if I could help with anything, passing fence after fence down and shingles everywhere. She has a large yard, and two large sections of fence were laying on the ground. I was surprised to see one section of the fence sitting untouched, and a little tree about three or four yards in front of it was completely untouched. It was spring, and the white buds on the young tree were all still pretty; it was as if nothing at all had happened that day. It had been totally protected.

We had financial protection as well, for although insurance covered most of the expenses, others had to pay their deductible and depreciation share of costs. In our area, those costs are often between five and six thousand dollars that insurance will not pay. The homeowners were now looking at that unexpected expense. We were very blessed to have been protected.

"Nor the pestilence that stalks in the darkness, nor the plague that destroys at midday" (Psalm 91:6).

A pestilent disease is extremely destructive or harmful. Once again, in this verse, protection from disease is mentioned. Also, once again, midday disasters are mentioned. When God repeats Himself, as He has here, this is so we will truly hear and understand. We need to know this: Epidemic diseases may come, but God said twice in these verses that we will be okay. Disasters will come, but twice God tells us He sees, and we are protected.

 This reminds me of a story my mom told me that happened when I was a baby.

The sirens in Plano, Texas, where we lived didn't sound, but there was a storm going on that woke me up, I guess, and scared me. Mom said I was crying, so she came up to put me back to sleep and stayed with me in the room. There was a huge window in the room, not far from my crib. My parents were surprised the next morning to find out that a tornado had gone through their neighborhood and nearby neighborhoods. A row of pretty trees in the middle of one of the main streets had been blown down. There was a great deal of damage. Businesses had to be closed that day due to the damage. It could have been horrible, but we were protected.

This story came to Carlisle's memory as soon as she read verse 6. Our daughter-in-law, Jessica, teaches their children the stories of

God's miracles in their family. It is important to let our children know how real God's protection is.

"A thousand may fall at your side, and ten thousand at your right hand. But it will not come near you" (Psalm 91:7).

Do you see why booklets of Psalm 91 are distributed to our military? We don't know all they see while fighting on the front lines. They for sure need to know where to find safety. Where is that? It is in the shadow of the Most High.

 I have another story. This reminds me of how God protected my grandfather, my mom's dad. It was 9/11, and the towers in New York had fallen because of those two planes. A third plane had flown into the Pentagon, where my grandfather was at work, and the spot where it hit was exactly where my grandfather's office was. But that whole section was closed because remodeling was going on, and he and other coworkers were safely working on the other side of the Pentagon in a temporary office. God works in simple but miraculous ways. Probably nobody was thinking that having an office remodeled would save a life. But that's what God did.

Once again, we see that Tom and Jessica have continued to teach their girls about God and His loving protection. These stories came to her mind just at the mention of these verses. If you are doing that too, how wonderful. If not, you can start now. Watch God at work, study His word with your children, pray with them. This will help them be alert to God's movements on their behalf.

"You will only observe with your eyes and see the punishment of the wicked" (Psalm 91:8).

What was meant to harm us is now turned back to the enemy. Watch God punish our enemies. Listen for stories like this. We only have to read the Bible and look around, and we can see that God punishes our enemies. God cannot let sin go without consequences.

If it seems like they are getting away with the wrong they have done, according to Scripture, it is only a matter of time. Don't take matters into your own hands. Vengeance is God's, says the Word (Romans12:19), and this verse 8 says that we will only observe with our eyes.

"If you make the Most High your dwelling—even the Lord, who is my refuge—then no harm will befall you, no disaster will come near your tent" (Psalm 91:9–10).

This says "if you," while some translations say "because you." There is something we must do to receive this. It doesn't just happen. What do we have to do? We can't ignore this small word *if* in this scripture. We have to make the Lord our safe place.

The Shadow of the Most High

Verse 1 says, "He who lives in the shadow of the Most High." This implies that not all live there. But those of us who choose to live there are promised this protection. That is how the chapter started out in verse 1. Here it says because we do this, nothing will hurt us. No trouble will come near us. Abiding there, in that safe place, we wake up right there by our heavenly Father.

Do you greet God? Do you start the day with Him? Do you have worship songs you like to sing to Him, praises to give to Him with thanksgiving for watching over you as you slept?

What about praising Him for lovely things happening to you or your family? God loves to sing with you, and He has often taken over a song as I sing the melody.

(Forgive us, Lord, for the many mornings we neglected to even acknowledge you when waking up. Thank you for making us aware of this.)

Kendall remembered a wonderful story. Let her tell it to you:

A Popsicle Saves a Life: God Works in Mysterious Ways

Kendall shared an amazing story with me about a classmate's grandfather. Her friend's grandfather was on vacation in Mexico. As he looked out his hotel window, he saw a man selling popsicles. A popsicle would taste good, he thought, so he went down the elevator and outside to buy one. Suddenly, there was a massive earthquake, and the hotel collapsed. God protected Kendall's friend's grandfather simply by making him hungry for a popsicle, and in time to get down the elevator and outside the building before the earthquake happened.

Kendall's story reminded me of something that happened when Bob was in the military, and we were stationed in Germany. We were at a football game, watching our son David play. The bleachers were full of parents and children, and some children were playing beneath the bleachers. The mother of the children under the bleachers sent her children to the snack bar for a drink and snack. Her children were at the snack bar window when suddenly the bleachers collapsed. Had those children still been under the bleachers, they would have been badly hurt or killed. We were in the stands across the field, and it was a strange sight to see a whole stand full of people suddenly disappear before our eyes. People were shaken up, but no injuries were reported. Only God could have seen to that.

"For he will command his angels concerning you to guard you in all your ways" (Psalm 91:11).

We can go to school, to work, on a vacation, to a friend's home. Our angels are assigned to make sure we are in this armor of shelter and protection. Just picture this and smile.

 Grammy, when I'm afraid, I reach out for God's hand. I am afraid in the dark, but when I must walk across a dark room, I reach out both of my hands for God and Jesus. Then I look behind me to see the

Holy Spirit, look above me, and know my two angels are there. I am surrounded by five powerful protectors.

One time when I was doing this, my mom was there and asked, "What are you doing?" "Holding God's hand," I said with a smile.

Carli's story makes me smile, for I can just picture all of that. I've since grabbed for God's hand if facing something that makes me nervous.

Talking about something that makes anyone nervous, it's the sound of the unmistakable rattle of the tail of a rattlesnake. I've heard it one time, and it was when Tom was ten. We were living at Edwards Air Force Base, where Bob was stationed at the time. That is in the Mojave Desert in California where the space shuttles practiced their landings on the dry lake bed. That was in the early 1980s.

Tom and I had just gotten out of the car and were walking forward in the dark. Suddenly, we heard the sound of the rattlesnake. I told him to walk backwards and get back in the car, which we safely did. Because it was dark, I have no idea how close we were to that rattlesnake, and I don't want to know. It was a sound I have never forgotten. I thank God that we were safe.

This is a story that just happened to a friend of mine. This true story will clearly testify that verse 11 is a fact about angels guarding our ways. Melvin Pillay and his wife Michele were driving from Arizona to California. They had driven a hundred miles and decided to get out to stretch their legs. Their little dog Raja was with them, so they set him down on the ground. Melvin and Michele were talking while watching Raja meander about. Raja was about five feet away from him when Mel heard that sound of a rattlesnake. He looked past Raja, and a foot and a half past this fourteen-pound dog was a coiled, hissing rattlesnake. His tail was rattling, and his fangs were out. He was poised to strike.

Melvin said that he never felt so hopeless and so helpless in his life. He couldn't run toward Raja, for he often played that way and Raja would run right into the rattlesnake. Melvin was five feet away and Raja was still meandering about. Now he was less than a foot from the snake. Raja had never seen a snake in his life and was just walking and sniffing the ground as dogs do.

Suddenly, Melvin said that something rose up in his spirit, and he felt as though something came out of his spirit. "I felt my spirit call out to God, and I felt a breakthrough. Michele called, 'Jesus!' Raja stopped and looked at Michele. We were still one hundred miles from a hospital, and we knew no veterinarians in this area. In less than five seconds, I ran, picked up Raja, and the worst thing that could happen to someone rescuing their pet happened. My flip-flop slipped off, tripping me. Now I was falling forward, with my dog in my arms, toward the snake. I was looking into the snake's eyes, when suddenly I fell back a few feet, landing pretty violently, but away from the snake. I got up, and we got in the car. We were thanking God for the protection. As I thought about it, I said to Michele that I marveled that I fell backwards instead of landing on the snake. Michele said, 'Mel, you didn't fall backwards, you flew backwards about five feet. It was though you were knocked backwards, as if something hit you out of the way.'"

Melvin's hand was bleeding from the rough landing, but he said that he was not in any pain. You can think what you want; I think that an angel knocked Melvin, as he was falling forward, back with such a force that he landed on his back instead of landing on top of the snake.

Melvin said, "Something was going on between the natural and the supernatural. As I was thanking God for this protection, suddenly I heard the words of my morning prayer clearly rise up. I had prayed that God would keep His hand upon us, protecting us as we traveled. Don't ever think that prayer isn't effective. I was calling Raja, but my spirit was calling to God, speaking to God, releasing that angel to react instantly. The feeling and sensations of those few seconds, I can't even begin to describe."

Cool testimony.

Incredible testimony.

I can't even imagine what that would feel like experiencing that.

Fear, horror, amazement? I don't think I want to find out. I know I don't want to find out.

The Policeman Was Still Sorting out What He Had Witnessed

Delores Neblett, one of the leaders of a Bible study I attend, gave me permission to share this story:

Dee was at a stop sign at a four-way intersection. She had arrived first, and then cars arrived at each of the other three stop signs. Having the right of way, she started through the intersection, but the lady on her right moved to come through. Dee saw her and accelerated as fast as she could, hoping to avoid the other woman's car. But she clipped the lady's car, spinning her, and Dee found herself airborne. She went over a tree, over a hedge, and the car was set down on the other side of the hedge.

A policeman who happened to be at the scene came to her window and asked if she was okay.

"Yes," Dee replied, "but I don't know what happened."

The policeman said, "Your car was at the stop sign, and now it sits here on the other side of a tree and a hedge—and I watched it all. It was as if your car was lifted out of harm's way and set down safely."

The other woman was not injured. The policeman, Dee told us, didn't give a ticket to either of them, for he was still sorting out the miracle he had witnessed.

"They will lift you up in their hands, so that you will not strike your foot against a stone" (Psalm 91:12).

Okay, I had a talk with God about this verse over twenty years ago. (Yes, I confess I can have a little attitude at times.) One day when we lived in San Antonio, I was enjoying my usual prayer time while walking our dogs. I tell this story in *Restore, Restore, Restore and More*, my first book.

So this prayer time had become a very important mountain-moving time, and I am not exaggerating. I decided to use this time to also clean up the streets of San Antonio of discarded aluminum cans. So I was walking, praying, and picking up cans.

(Do you already see the problem here?)

I spotted a can down in a drainage ditch. I started down, slipped on a rock, and landed so hard that I felt the discs in my spine compressing all the way up to my neck.

I was praying when I fell, and I indignantly told God, "I know there is a verse that angels will hold me up if I slip on a stone; they didn't, and that hurt! And I was talking to You."

I heard the Holy Spirit say that I had just had my breath knocked out of me, there are no broken bones, and that I would be better in a minute.

It wasn't long, and I was able to breathe again and get up. Shaken, I staggered home with the dogs and asked Tom to drive me to the ER. My hands were numb, so the ER staff thought some serious damage had been done. X-rays showed all was fine, but it was three months before I healed from the terrible fall. The hard fall tore cartilage away from my rib cage, and that had to heal.

I learned then that God is indeed a jealous God, as He has written in His Word in Exodus 20:5, 34:19; Deuteronomy 4:24; and 2 Corinthians 11:2. Years before God led me to that prayer time while walking with our dog, and it was our time. He had warned me through the scriptures to not be lukewarm about my time with Him, but my focus had shifted from God and our fellowship to recycling aluminum cans. I was not protected by Psalm 91, because I was not living in the shelter of the Most High, but in the world.

You can see, Grammy, the world is not the best shelter. Leave God time God time and can time can time.

I gave up picking up cans a long, long time ago. I learned my lesson.

"You will tread on the lion and the cobra; you will trample the great lion and the serpent" (Psalm 91:13).

Daniel spent an entire night in a den full of lions, and he was unharmed. Carlisle pointed out that this was truly a miracle, for she read that those thrown into lion's dens were torn apart before hitting the ground.

Paul picked up a log with a venomous snake on it. It bit him, and he shook it off and was fine.

One day, my dog, Bo, and I unknowingly were walking side by side with a venomous snake, and we were unharmed. Only God could have done that. I actually had been warned by the Holy Spirit to watch out for a snake, so I had been walking, praying, and watching out for that snake. After having walked and not seen anything for about thirty or forty minutes, I forgot about the snake and was just praying. I stepped onto a wooden bridge that spans the lake, with Bo right beside me. Glancing down, I saw this thick water moccasin right beside Bo, slithering toward the water. The snake was about six inches from Bo. Only God could have kept a curious dog and a poisonous snake apart. Bo and I walk this pretty path often, and I thank God each time I step onto the bridge for this protection miracle.

"'Because he loves me,' says the Lord, 'I will rescue him; I will protect him, for he acknowledges my name'" (Psalm 91:14).

Here is that word again, "because" (or it might say "if" in your Bible). Because you are in love with God. Are you? If so, God will bring you out of trouble. Do you know God's name? Then God will have His angels set you on a safe place. Again, it is up to us to do our part.

 This is kind of like you have an issue with something, but because God loves you He'll bring you out of the trouble. If you don't pay attention to Him, He'll have to discipline you. That is only because He loves you and wants the best for you.

"He will call upon Me, and I will answer him. I will be with him in trouble. I will take him out of trouble and honor him" (Psalm 91:15).

This translation says, "He will call" (call upon God), meaning any of us can do that. Other translations say, "When we will call." When we call upon God; is that name at the tip of your tongue? Do you call upon God? We should be calling on Him when we're happy. We should be calling on Him when we are afraid. Either way, God will answer you. If you are happy, God would love to hear you tell Him. If you are in trouble, He wants to get you out of there. Call Him, and there He is.

Do you have your verses memorized through verse 15? One more to go. Keep working on it.

"With long life I will satisfy him and show him my salvation" (Psalm 91:16).

Psalm 91 promises that our days won't be cut short by enemy plots, deadly diseases, or premature death. We are sticking with God, seeking refuge under His wings. We are listening to His stories about how others actually experienced this protection, and this builds our faith.

That's God Talking to Us

That's God talking to us through the Bible. That's a wonderful promise. Yet some people don't focus on God. What an incredible saving power God is. Don't overlook these wonderful miracles God gives us every day. Don't think of these things as nothing: the air we breathe, our families that love us. Don't waste the gift of another day that God gives you.

Carli is so right, and I thank her for reminding us.

Let me pause here and extend an invitation. Carlisle and I would love to hear your stories. You can share them with us by going to the Ann Lynn Noble Facebook page and posting your stories there. Readers, feel free to read them there as well. Sharing our stories will be fantastic.

My stories range from over twenty years ago to as recent as a few months ago (the one about the snake—ugh! I so don't like snakes). Yours can be recent or from some time ago.

Carlisle has a story from when she was a baby. It was told by her parents and was about her grandfather being protected on 9/11, before she was even born. I know you must have stories to share, as well.

Please write and share your story with us.

Powerful and Effective
Prayers of Children

Do not be anxious about anything, but in every situation, by
prayer and petition, with thanksgiving, present your requests to
God. And the peace of God, which transcends all understanding,
will guard your hearts and your minds in Christ Jesus.

—Philippians 4:6–7 (NIV)

I am very, very impressed with the power of a child's prayer. You
will be too, after I share this story.

Our son Tom, Jessica, and the girls were gone for a week, and
we were caring for Maxie, their sweet ten-year-old Brittany. We had
a doggie door, so she was in and out on her own.

It was a Sunday morning, and we were getting ready for church.
Our dog Bo was in the house, but I didn't see Maxie. I checked
outside to see what she was doing, and I noticed the gate was wide
open. (We learned later that someone thought it would be fun to
open all the gates in our neighborhood during the night.)

I snapped the leash on Bo and started searching for Maxie. Bob
got in the car and started driving around. Golfers were starting to
play on the golf course, so I put them on alert. Maxie was nowhere
to be seen. Bob had no luck, either.

I texted Jessica and told her to get the girls and pray because Maxie was missing. Two minutes later, at the most, Jessica called and said Maxie had been found. Maxie had the phone number of a pet registration agency on her collar. The agency had just called Jessica and had given her the phone number of the man who found her.

I called the man, who happened to be the one who delivers our newspaper. He had found Maxie in a field outside our neighborhood, heading in the direction he was driving. On Sundays, he delivers the papers between four and five o'clock in the morning, so Maxie had to have escaped early that morning and had been roaming around. She had to go under a brick wall around our gated community to get into that field, but there are places that was possible for a small dog. That kind man had stopped his car, walked out into the field, and picked her up. Seeing the number on her collar to call, he had done just that. A coincidence that Maxie was there as this man drove by that field, and that it was light enough by then that he even saw her? I think not. I believe it was God's grace and plan to answer a prayer these girls would pray. Before the prayer, God had the answer all ready. What a lesson for us to be encouraged to pray about everything.

He was in front of our house with Maxie before Bob could collect Bo and me and drive back home. So five minutes after those girls prayed, Maxie was safely back in our house, exhausted from her escapade.

As a result of answered prayer, their faith soared levels higher. Mine did, as well. I was in awe, as I always am when God moves. When Carli says she is praying for me, I feel so covered. God is listening to children and sends teams of angels to answer their prayers.

The girls have three or four more stories, so their job as coauthors is to write them out for us. I can't wait to read them.

Maxie died at age fourteen, and our family missed her so much that we bought a new Brittany puppy that looked just like Maxie. We named her Pepper.

Not long after that, we bought another Brittany

that needed to be rescued, and we needed her to be a playmate for Pepper. We named this one Coco. Unfortunately, these two puppies are just as much escape artists as Maxie was.

Let me tell you about this one time. We had met Grammy and Grandad for lunch and then ran some errands. The dogs were left in the backyard, and we were gone three hours. When we got home, I went to the door to let the puppies in. When I didn't see them, I went outside, glanced to my left, and saw the gate was open. Apparently, the yard man had not closed it tightly, and the dogs were able to escape.

I ran back in to tell everyone that the dogs were gone. In the rush, my mom told me to put some shoes on. I found some flip-flops and got in the car with my mom and Caitlin. (Flip-flops were not a wise idea, for we had to get out of the car to do some searching, and it was cold, wet, and muddy.) My dad was in the other car, driving around looking with Kendall. I told everyone we needed to stop and pray together. I prayed, "Dear Lord, thank you for this rain and cold, but we pray that You help us find these dogs like You helped us find Maxie."

Persevere in Prayer

After an hour with no success, we called Grammy and Grandad to ask for their help. They drove over with Bo in hopes the dogs would run to him. This was not a fast answer like Maxie, and thoughts were going through my head that scared me. What if they were trapped or hurt by a car. I was very scared, so I just kept praying.

There was a lot of construction going on, and we asked the workmen building the new houses if they had seen them. They had not. The mail lady was driving down the street, so my mom pulled up beside her and asked if she had seen two dogs.

She said, "Actually, I did see two very wet dogs sitting on a hill up there, and I wondered what they were doing."

We described Pepper and Coco, and she said those were the ones she had seen.

That hill was beside some woods, which is a wildlife reserve. My dad went in there, and Caitlin and I ran up the street to help, with Grammy and Bo beside us. Mom got there too, and all but Grammy and Bo went into the woods. They stayed outside the fence in case the dogs came out alone. Kendall was with Grandad.

My dad found Pepper first, and it was good I was there, for I was able to get Coco and put a leash on her. My dad had to carry Pepper, because we didn't have another leash. Both dogs were muddy, cut, and full of brambles, which knotted their fur.

We were all so very cold. We got the dogs home and put them in the bathtub. My mom had to cut the knotted fur off, which was the only way to help them. They were exhausted, and we were as well. We thanked God that they were safe, and although they had cuts on them, they were not seriously hurt.

I actually could tell you more stories about these escape artist dogs, prayers, and safe returns, but I want to give you another example of our prayers at work.

We were building a new home, so our house was going to be for sale. We had two open houses, but only curious neighbors came. My sisters and I prayed that the house would be sold. The third open house resulted in more neighbors and one family outside the neighborhood. That one family loved our house and ended up buying it.

God knew just who He wanted in that house, someone who would love it as much as we did. Now we will be closer to Grammy and Grandad, and my parents have really good friends who live in our new neighborhood. The schools we will now be going to are very close to the house we are building, and one of them is brand new.

Prayer works.

I want to point out something. The prayer for Maxie was answered in five minutes. The other prayers were not answered as quickly, but they were answered. The girls persevered in prayer, somehow knowing God would come through in the end. God is teaching them while they are still children to persevere in prayer, something we all have to learn.

God loves when we pray it through and believe it through. How do I know? I felt God Himself told me so. It was as if He really wanted me to know that, for not long afterwards, it was then confirmed through a prophetic word. One of the teachers I taught with in the middle school had invited me to her church that evening. I had never met anyone with the gift of prophecy before. He was a man named Mike, in his late forties, a blond, and his beautiful blonde-haired twenty-year-old daughter was there, as well. She also had that gift, but it was her dad who was speaking. The prophet didn't know me at all, but this is what Mike said: "Ann, since you prayed it through and believed it through, God has chosen you to be head of a brand-new agency of faith." That was in 1996. Over all these years since, I have held onto that word without doubting, and I'm now seeing this new strategy God is moving in which I've was able to describe in my first book, *Restore, Restore, Restore and More.*

Encourage your children to pray and to keep believing and praying until the answer is seen. You all will be rewarded.

Oh, I almost forgot to remind you to keep a journal of all your children's prayers. As the answers come, find that prayer request and journal what God did. What a wonderful record of faith for your children to have. Please do that.

Chapter 4

Children and Health:
Fit, Healthy, and Happy

I prayed for a week before starting this chapter, for I had no idea what God would want to let us know about children and health. I asked Carlisle to pray too. Finally, the thoughts started flowing, and we wrote them down.

Healing Is the Children's Bread

Children know what health looks like, and they expect it. See, health is our inheritance. Jesus told us that He took care of sickness on the cross. God wants us healthy. It should be expected. Sometimes, even children have something go wrong healthwise. But remember, they are equipped with that pure childlike faith that can tackle anything. God wants to put this to work. God wants to put children and their faith into action on this battlefield.

About twenty-five years ago, I was at a Christian conference. One of the speakers relayed this story when it was her turn to speak. Earlier, she had been sitting in the audience very much in pain with a stiff neck. She sat there, miserable, wondering how she was going to get through her presentation. Suddenly, a little girl with Down syndrome sitting behind her put her hand on the speaker's neck in the exact place it hurt and said, "I wuv you." Heat went through her, the nerve was released, and she was totally healed. God used that little girl to heal that speaker.

What do we need to do to help our children be successful in this mission from God?

First of all, armor. People going onto a battlefield put on their armor. When I taught in a Christian school in the Chicago area, we would act out putting on our armor each morning before we started the day. If I happened to forget, my students never did. I would see a hand go up, and then I would hear, "Mrs. Noble, can we put on our armor?" You see, it makes a noticeable difference. That is why God gives the gift of armor to us.

The Armor of God

Every morning, I look at myself in the mirror, and I act out putting on my armor, the armor of God. Then I salute God and walk out, fully ready to start the day.

What is our armor? Ephesians 6:13–17 explains it (this is the NIV translation):

"Finally, be strong in the Lord and in his mighty power. Put on the full armor of God, so that you can take your stand against the devil's schemes. For our struggle is not against flesh and blood, but against the rulers, against the authorities, against the powers of this dark world and against the spiritual forces of evil in the heavenly realms. Therefore put on the full armor of God, so that when the day of evil comes, you may be able to stand your ground, and after you have done everything, to stand. Stand firm then, with the belt of truth buckled around your waist, with the breastplate of righteousness in place, and with your feet fitted with the readiness that comes from the gospel of peace. In addition to all this, take up the shield of faith, with which you can extinguish all the flaming arrows of the evil one. Take the helmet of salvation and the sword of the Spirit, which is the word of God."

Using my classroom armor exercises as an example, we first put on our helmet of salvation. A soldier's helmet protects his head from deadly blows, and the helmet of salvation protects the mind against anything that would disconnect us from our spiritual walk with the Lord.

Next comes the breastplate of righteousness, to protect our heart. With the breastplate of righteousness in place, our hearts are protected against accusations Satan might make against us. We have an identity through Christ, but Satan likes to convince us differently. The breastplate of righteousness keeps thoughts Satan tries to implant in our hearts from getting in. Our son-in-law is a deputy sheriff in San Antonio, and every day, he puts on bulletproof vest before going to work. Think of the breastplate of righteousness as a bulletproof vest to protect our heart from Satan's fiery darts. That bulletproof vest is necessary for Jarrod to be protected as he works, and God said this invisible armor is necessary for us just to live out each day. Like Jarrod, we must remember to put it all on.

We buckle the belt of truth around our waist. This truth we learn from the Bible lets us know how to avoid dangerous traps and how to stay on the safe path that God wants us on. It's important to have this belt of truth securely around our waist. Read the Bible with your children. Help them to learn verses they can use in situations. There are so many promises of God in the Bible for us to stand on in prayer. Read that Bible daily.

To protect our feet against stepping on Satan's traps, we put on the sandals of peace. These sandals of peace remind us that Jesus says nothing or nobody can snatch us out of His hands; therefore, we keep our firm foundation in Christ.

We gird our loins with the strength of God, like tucking in any long or loose clothing that would interfere while we are running. Jesus is our strength.

It is important that we take up the double-edge sword of the Spirit, which is scripture and prayer. In my classroom, at that point, we pretended to pull a sword out of our belt. Both sides of the sword are important, so we back our prayer with promises from the Word of God.

Finally, we pick up the big shield of that wonderful gift of faith, which protects us from the fiery darts Satan hurls at us.

All of this armor is a perfect and wonderful gift from God. Please, don't leave it at home. Don't run out without it. Leave a note to yourself or a picture of it found in the Bible. I'm talking to myself as well as to you.

Did you know that Jesus even put on that armor before a battle?

"He saw that there was no one, he was appalled that there was no one to intervene; so his own arm achieved salvation for him, and his own righteousness sustained him. He put on righteousness as his breastplate, and the helmet of salvation on his head; he put on the garments of vengeance and wrapped himself in zeal as in a cloak" (Isaiah 59:16–17 NIV).

Each morning, having put on our gift of the armor of God, we are ready to pray and to intercede in prayer.

Carlisle has a story she will tell of how their prayers were badly needed for a very sick friend.

 Grammy wanted you to know about my classmate, so I will start with telling you that I was home with a stomach bug, and when I came back to school, Noah wasn't there. Everyone was kind of sad, so I asked them, "Why are you so sad?" They were like, well, "You see who isn't here. Noah is in the hospital."

I said, "What?" And so they explained to me that apparently, he had a mass on his brain and had to be rushed to the kid's hospital because he was throwing up so badly. All this was going on while I was home sick.

I asked them what happened, and they said they didn't really know how he got the mass on the brain, but he was in the hospital. Apparently, there was something pushing on his brain. If it pushed too hard, it might go through his blood veins, like a blood clot, except in your brain. It's called a mass on your brain, I guess. They didn't really know how to help him, but we all did. The whole school prayed every single day for him each morning—in all of our classes in the school, not just ours. His picture was posted in the hallway to remind us to pray on our own, as well.

The doctors thought they might have to do surgery. We thought Noah was getting surgery on his brain. Apparently, however, they didn't have to do surgery at this time because he was getting better. They figured out that he really was healing, so they just had to give him rest. If he heard loud noises, his head would hurt. He would get a serious migraine. Therefore, he couldn't stay the full school day. If he did, he was really tired.

We made him a blanket, and it was one of those knot blankets. Each knot we tied, we each got to say a little prayer and make a video. We sent it to Noah while he was still resting at home.

But, yeah, they didn't have to do the surgery, which was amazing. It was an answer to all of our prayers, for we were so praying that he didn't have to have surgery.

That not having to have surgery was really amazing, and when they told us he could soon come back to school, we were so excited.

Noah got better and better, and the first day he came back to school, we were really excited, and he was fine. It was like nothing had happened.

Day after day, he would just get stronger and stronger. It was amazing that God healed him so fast, for stuff like that some people have to have surgery and are never the same again. Our friend is just perfectly fine now, which is really a miracle.

This is how God is using children to pray. This is not new, for children have always been strong prayer warriors. Children pray from their heart. They pray boldly, sure that God hears their prayers. They are honest in their prayers and willingly pray. Now there seems to be a stronger-than-ever anointing on more children, and the evidence of that is being seen.

As Carlisle explained to us, a very serious problem was stopped and turned around. They saw Noah's strength coming back right before their eyes. They didn't know it, but when the school got together in unity of agreement that God would heal their friend, along with the power of their corporate prayers, they were unstoppable in making that mountain move off Noah. They didn't know that was going on; they were just praying for Noah. They expected it would work, and it did.

I want these children praying for my needs, don't you? I can see children in hospitals being supernaturally healed, then getting up and running from room to room, laying healing hands on other children. I am totally expecting that to happen and see hospital rooms emptying.

We Can't Limit God

"But will God really dwell on earth? The heavens, even the highest heaven, cannot contain you. How much less this temple I have built!" (1 Kings 8:27 NIV).

We definitely can't limit God. This verse tells us our God is huge. We put limits on Him with our own mind, our own beliefs. God tells us not to lean on our own understanding. Our own understanding can't think big enough for God, nor can it know the best way you should go.

"Trust in the LORD with all your heart and lean not on your own understanding; in all your ways submit to him, and he will make your paths straight" (Proverbs 3:5–6 NIV).

We are not the first generations to have this problem. Look at Matthew 8:26. Jesus was talking to his disciples.

"He replied, 'You of little faith, why are you so afraid?' Then he got up and rebuked the winds and the waves, and it was completely calm. The men were amazed and asked, 'What kind of man is this? Even the winds and the waves obey him!'" (Matthew 8:26–27 NIV).

What were they afraid of? We have to back up to verses 23–25 to find out.

Jesus Calms the Storm

"Then he got into the boat and his disciples followed him. Suddenly a furious storm came up on the lake, so that the waves swept over the boat. But Jesus was sleeping. The disciples went and woke him, saying, 'Lord, save us! We're going to drown!'"

Jesus wasn't fearful of the storm. It says He was asleep. That verse lets us know Jesus was disappointed that they had no faith they would be safe with Him.

Here is a man who didn't disappoint Jesus. He amazed Jesus with his faith, in fact. Let's read about the centurion. One of his servants was suffering terribly, so he came to find Jesus.

"Jesus said to him, 'Shall I come and heal him?' The centurion replied, 'Lord, I do not deserve to have you come under my roof. But just say the word, and my servant will be healed. For I myself am a man under authority, with soldiers under me. I tell this one, "Go," and he goes; and that one, "Come," and he comes. I say to my servant, "Do this," and he does it.' When Jesus heard this, he was amazed and said to those following him, 'Truly I tell you, I have not found anyone in Israel with such great faith'" (Matthew 8:7–10 NIV).

What a huge compliment the centurion received. Wouldn't you like to hear Jesus say that about you? We can, if we just believe what our heavenly Father says.

Think about it. God created the heavens and the earth by just speaking it into being. I love to read Genesis chapter 1.

Do you remember the day God made Adam? If you were a

student in a Christian school, you would study Genesis and there would be a test about what God created on each of those six days. I know, because I taught third and fourth grades in a Christian school when we lived in the Chicago area. Let's read it and see if you could pass that test.

God Spoke, the Holy Spirit Moved, and God Saw It Was Good

The Beginning

"In the beginning God created the heavens and the earth. Now the earth was formless and empty, darkness was over the surface of the deep, and the Spirit of God was hovering over the waters.

"And God said, 'Let there be light,' and there was light. God saw that the light was good, and he separated the light from the darkness. God called the light 'day,' and the darkness he called 'night.' And there was evening, and there was morning—the first day.

"And God said, 'Let there be a vault between the waters to separate water from water.' So God made the vault and separated the water under the vault from the water above it. And it was so. God called the vault 'sky.' And there was evening, and there was morning—the second day.

"And God said, 'Let the water under the sky be gathered to one place, and let dry ground appear.' And it was so. God called the dry ground 'land,' and the gathered waters he called 'seas.' And God saw that it was good.

"Then God said, 'Let the land produce vegetation: seed-bearing plants and trees on the land that bear fruit with seed in it, according to their various kinds.' And it was so. The land produced vegetation: plants bearing seed according to their kinds and trees bearing fruit with seed in it according to their kinds. And God saw that it was good. And there was evening, and there was morning—the third day.

"And God said, 'Let there be lights in the vault of the sky to separate the day from the night, and let them serve as signs to mark sacred times, and days and years, and let them be lights in the vault of the sky to give light on the earth.' And it was so. God made two great lights—the greater light to govern the day and the lesser light to govern the night. He also made the stars. God set them in the vault of the sky to give light on the earth, to govern the day and the night, and to separate light from darkness. And God saw that it was good. And there was evening, and there was morning—the fourth day.

"And God said, 'Let the water teem with living creatures, and let birds fly above the earth across the vault of the sky.' So God created the great creatures of the sea and every living thing with which the water teems and that moves about in it, according to their kinds, and every winged bird according to its kind. And God saw that it was good. God blessed them and said, 'Be fruitful and increase in number and fill the water in the seas, and let the birds increase on the earth.' And there was evening, and there was morning—the fifth day.

"And God said, 'Let the land produce living creatures according to their kinds: the livestock, the creatures that move along the ground, and the wild animals, each according to its kind.' And it was so. God made the wild animals according to their kinds, the livestock according to their kinds, and all the creatures that move along the ground according to their kinds. And God saw that it was good.

"Then God said, 'Let us make mankind in our image, in our likeness, so that they may rule over the fish in the sea and the birds in the sky, over the livestock and all the wild animals, and over all the creatures that move along the ground.'

"So God created mankind in his own image, in the image of God he created them; male and female he created them.

"God blessed them and said to them, 'Be fruitful and increase in number; fill the earth and subdue it. Rule over the fish in the sea and the birds in the sky and over every living creature that moves on the ground.'

"Then God said, 'I give you every seed-bearing plant on the face of the whole earth and every tree that has fruit with seed in it. They will be yours for food. And to all the beasts of the earth and all the birds in the sky and all the creatures that move along the ground—everything that has the breath of life in it—I give every green plant for food.' And it was so.

"God saw all that he had made, and it was very good. And there was evening, and there was morning—the sixth day" (Genesis 1:1–31 NIV).

And what did God do on the seventh day? Yes, indeed: He rested.

Why would we limit Him?

Another thing, God knows the rotation of each planet as well of the names of all the stars.

"He determines the number of the stars and calls them each by name" (Psalm 147:4 NIV).

Do you know how many stars are in the universe? Well, I wish I knew the answer to this question, but not only do I not know, no one does. Even so, this question brings up amazing facts. NASA says that there are at least two hundred billion stars in the Milky Way galaxy alone. The Bible says God knows each of their names.

Why would we limit Him?

Here is something else to think about. The Bible tells us that God keeps a book about each and every one of us. That means each and every person who walked on the earth. I didn't make that up. I'll show you the verses.

"And I saw the dead, great and small, standing before the throne, and books were opened. Another book was opened, which is the book of life. The dead were judged according to what they had done as recorded in the books" (Revelation 20:12 NIV).

"For we must all appear before the judgment seat of Christ, so that each of us may receive what is due us for the things done while in the body, whether good or bad" (2 Corinthians 5:10 NIV).

Children are increasingly getting words of knowledge and healing gifts. (We will devote another chapter to the gifts of the Holy Spirit found in the Bible.) Expect to see miracles and supernatural healings, turning these sweet children into fit, healthy, and happy models of God's abundant grace, mercy, and power.

Why would we ever think of limiting Him?

Children and Relationships: Happy Home, Happy Life

Some parents I know have, or had, prodigal children. God has more prodigal children than stars in the sky. He talks about us in His Word: "We all, like sheep, have gone astray, each of us has turned to our own way" (Isaiah 53:6 NIV). God had to deal with this, so He did it by laying this sin of ours on His own Son on the cross. This was very hard on Jesus, but He didn't open His mouth. He took the punishment we should have received for not following God and going our own way. Extreme, yes, but God loves us children that much.

What about our children and God? I will tell you what I found out talking to Carlisle.

I told her chapter 5 is about our relationships. Carli immediately said, "With God!"

As the saying goes, she hit the nail on the head. She was exactly right. The relationship is the one with God. That has to be correct first before any other relationship will work.

I asked Carli to tell us what she felt about her relationship at her age with God.

My relationship with God is better now than when I was younger, and I believe everyone will mature over time as I did. For me personally, I was not that close to God when I was little. I mean, I thought about God; I went to church; I knew Who God was, but I didn't completely grasp just what having a relationship with God should be like. Then I went through fifth and sixth grades, and in fifth grade, something happened. I don't even know how to explain it, but I'll give it my best shot.

I go to a Christian school, and my Bible teacher just got so excited each time she was teaching us. It made it exciting to go to Bible class. Before, with my other teachers, we would still learn things, but everyone would be bored. I wasn't being taught in a way that really got to me.

I don't know what happened as I learned from this teacher, but I am just going to say it was a miracle. Now, when I am afraid about something, I talk with God. An example is when my grandfather had to get a CT scan and was waiting for the results. They would be good or bad, but I already prayed so I knew it was going to be okay. Most people don't have that comfort, knowing that God's always there for you, but I do.

See that faith of a child shine through? I did, as I typed what she had written. She had prayed, so she knew it was okay. God was there for her. His answer would be that it was good. There was no thought of *I hope that He hears me* or *Will it be okay?* She said she knew it would be okay, for God had this. He was there for her, and He heard her prayer.

No wonder God wants all of us to reach Him with our childlike faith. So strong, so sure.

This special teacher, by the way, was the subject of a writing contest Carlisle entered in sixth grade. She wrote how her Bible teaching impacted her life, and Carli won the contest. There are great teachers out there.

Relationship Starts with God and Me

Relationship starts with that God/me relationship. He and I. God and me. God and you. It starts there, and then it just flows, for the love of God is so very strong that it can't be contained inside of us. We reach out to others. We make friends. I made a friend who became my best friend, and I married him. Bob and I have been married fifty-two years as of August 7, 2017. We started out as best friends.

Children come in all ages. We children of God are all ages. Just because you find yourself in your seventies, as I am, doesn't mean that God doesn't think of us as His children.

God wants us to ask for wisdom. He wants His wisdom in us, guiding us as parents to raise our children in the right way. Proverbs 22:15 teaches us that a youngster's heart is filled with foolishness, but physical discipline drives it far away.

I wasn't even born yet, but this story about my older brother comes to mind. My mother and four-year-old Tommy were in a greenhouse. She looked around and didn't see him. Something prompted her to look up, and there he was: on top of the glass, smiling at her. He had no idea of the consequences had the greenhouse glass broken. She safely coaxed him down and then punished him. She loved him too much to not discipline him, the same as God loves us too much not to discipline us. Proverbs 3:11–12 tells us God disciplines out of love.

Unfortunately, we can't model common sense and expect it to transfer. We are all given common sense from God. Proverbs 10 tells us that several times.

I have observed three types of children in my seventy-six years. All three have something in common, and that one thing is that God loves them and has wonderful plans for their lives.

One of the child types is a wise child. A wise child pleases God and is blessed by God.

The second type is the prodigal child, who is bent to wander, a disposition that can sometimes be seen by the age of ten. These types of children are very hard to raise. You love them, but you don't like the way they behave. They start young and continue rebellious behavior into their teens and young adult years.

God allows consequences, not blessings, for the prodigal child. If you have been praying for them, they finally look up. The miracle turnaround finally occurs, but it was due only to God. Only God can take those children and set them on His purposed path, but through prayer, He certainly does.

The last type is one who has been raised in the Lord, loves the Lord, and is grounded in faith. Off to college you send them, with not a worry in your heart, and only later hear that Satan found a weak spot and dragged them into a trap. It is full of consequences. Tough love has to be given, and it works.

Prayer and God bring on the miracles. God let us see wonderful miracles while Bob and I raised our own children, blessing us with three amazingly strong adults who walk with the Lord.

You see, God wants us to walk in our purpose. He is counting on each of us to do our part for the kingdom of God. Sometimes, God has set up divine connections with people, and Satan tries all he can to stop that from happening.

Here is a true example of when a fourteen-year-old boy intervened, setting the stage for spiritual growth in my life. Bob had just been transferred from Ramstein Air Force Base in Germany back to the States, to Kelly Air Force Base in San Antonio, Texas. We were in our early forties then. At that time, our lives were so busy that we needed household help. Nubia Berrios came with such glowing references that we hired her. Nubia is a strong Christian woman, younger than I am, but when we met, she was very mature spiritually. She had raised her son to hear from God. She gave me permission to share this story with you.

Our relationship was really rocky at first. No matter what I did for Nubia, it never seemed right. She seemed miserable while in our home, and I was confused as to how to make things right. Nubia told her fourteen-year-old son that she was quitting. "No," he said with such authority that she knew that one word was from the Lord.

Then she realized that it was the enemy doing everything possible to see that we didn't stay connected. To make a long story short, Nubia was with us all seventeen years we were in San Antonio, and she was my Christian mentor. I love her like a sister. I am who I am today because of her mentoring. The point is that God used her teenage son to speak to his mother to make sure our relationship grew.

Love and Marriage

Another relationship God loves is marriage between a man and a woman. Today, fewer and fewer marriages last. What is happening? The Holy Spirit led me to understand it this way: They go their own way; they go away from God. They are on their own path trying to make things work, and it is a struggle. There is conflict with their spouse. They are trying to make things work in their own power, and that is not going to happen.

Children who are in dysfunctional families need to be instructed in the ways of the Lord. Children who are not in a relationship with God, as is quite often the case in a dysfunctional home, start hanging with a foolish crowd and walk the wrong way. They don't have the power of God to guide them. Their common sense is somehow buried, and the pleasure of the moment rules their days and nights.

Young King Josiah should be an encouragement to children who have had a rough childhood. Josiah was Israel's last good king, but his father and grandfather both were evil. I assume his mother or grandmothers followed the Lord and taught Josiah well. He became king of Israel at the age of eight. He lived under the influence of a father and grandfather who were both far from God, yet at such a young age, Josiah was a big influence on Israel, for he sought after God. This shows us that God can definitely use young children for

His purpose, even those children coming from a home ruled by evil men.

Even in a godly home, there can be prodigal children. Here is what God did to the Prodigal Son in the Bible: He pressed hard enough on him that the boy thought about what he was doing. The young man realized the path he was on was leading nowhere, that the pigs he was taking care of ate better than he did, and the boy finally came home.

God is busy creating pressure on prodigal children, and I have heard countless reports of parents saying their son or daughter just showed back up at home. What a blessing.

God is at work restoring relationships by getting people to look up and see their need for God. When they look up, they find God and establish that right relationship that contains the super glue to hold people together.

Children taught about God know relationships begin with Him. I didn't realize that would even be obvious to them until I told Carlisle that this chapter was about relationships. Her immediate response was, "About our relationship with God?" She went on to say, "If God was talking about a relationship, it was obviously our relationship with Him."

Proverbs has lots of instructions about parenting children: "Bring up a child by teaching him the way he should go, and when he is old he will not turn away from it" (Proverbs 22:6 NLV).

We need to train children while there is hope, since we truly love them. God disciplines us because He loves us, and so we see we are to discipline our children because we love them.

God is moving now to bring families back together—restoring relationships. A friend in Illinois told me that her son just suddenly appeared home, after having been gone two years. He just showed up, and things seem to be going fine now. A woman I met through my first book told me that their son recently returned, resumed his walk with the Lord, and is interviewing for work. Indeed, God is restoring relationships.

Do you see a relationship that needs prayer? Pray a hedge of thorns around them so they can't interact with anyone else without getting pricked by the thorns. We get knowledge of hedges from Job 1:10. Satan accused God of having a hedge of protection around Job.

"Have you not put a hedge around him and his household and everything he has? You have blessed the work of his hands, so that his flocks and herds are spread throughout the land" (Job 1:10 NIV).

There is another kind of hedge, as well. It's that hedge of thorns. When a hedge of horns is put around you, you get pricked if you try to go anywhere other than where God will lead you. You can't get to another person for advice without getting poked with a thorn. You can only look up to God for the answer.

Let's look at scripture that talks about the hedge of thorns. There are two of them. The first is Proverbs 15:19:

"The way of the sluggard is blocked with thorns, but the path of the upright is a highway" (Proverbs 15:19 NIV).

This is obviously for the lazy person, the one who wants a free handout with no work. A hedge around that person makes the way rough. The person right with the Lord, walking in his or her full potential, has a smooth road, with no places blocked.

Now, let's check out the other scripture. That is found in Hosea 2:6:

"Therefore, I will block her path with thornbushes; I will wall her in so that she cannot find her way" (Hosea 2:6).

This is the verse to use to pray a hedge of thorns around a prodigal child who has gotten involved with bad company, become addicted to drugs or alcohol, just really on a downward spiral somehow. The hedge of thorns put on those prodigal children will block their paths; the relationships they are in just won't work, not just with one, but with all. They can't make anything work, and it makes them just want to go home.

This verse is also used on an unfaithful spouse. They return home to the one they made a covenant with through marriage.

Put that hedge of thorns around them. They get pricked if they try to look anywhere else but up or down (and down doesn't work, either). They *have* to look up. Then God will handle this. We would like it to be in our perfect timing, which is right now. However, it is always in God's perfect timing, which only He sees and understands.

The family unit is so important to children. Think back, and you may remember your greatest fear was losing a parent. When there is a divorce in a home, that must feel like there is a huge loss. Quite often, children are used as pawns to hurt the other parent. No longer is a child allowed to grow with the love of both parents, but rather becomes a pawn to hurt the other parent. It sounds just awful, but I could line up people I have seen this happen to, and you could hear it from their own lips. I have seen this too many times to know that it is the norm for too many divorced parents with children. It is terribly sad.

We teachers see the hurt, the tired eyes from crying in the night, the unkempt hair from a parent too drunk to take care of a child getting ready for school. Oh, it shows. You may not think it does, but it really does.

Chase Away the Little Foxes

God speaks of prevention for a divorce. Song of Solomon 2:15 tells us to get rid of the little foxes, the small problems, before they become big ones. This doesn't just pertain to marriage but for everything.

"Catch for us the foxes, the little foxes that ruin the vineyards, our vineyards that are in bloom" (Song of Solomon 2:15 NIV).

Applying this to a married couple teaches that the couple needs to watch for the little problems that pop up. Ignoring them is the worst, for they become very aggressive. The Bible says that they should be talked about and dealt with together. They chase them away together, and all is well.

Keep God at the center of your relationships, and if you are right with Him, His love shines through. This is an example for everyone and a blessing to your children.

Chapter 6

The Lost Coin:
I Can't Find It Anywhere

Carlisle and I looked at the next title God had for us, and she immediately said:

"I talk to God all the time, so if I can't find something, I ask Him. God will find it for me."

Kendall was with us, and she said, "I ask my mom if she has seen it, and if she hasn't, then I ask God. He always finds it."

Ten Valuable Coins

The Parable of the Lost Coin

"Or suppose a woman has ten silver coins and loses one. Doesn't she light a lamp, sweep the house and search carefully until she finds it? And when she finds it, she calls her friends and neighbors together and says, 'Rejoice with me; I have found my lost coin'" (Luke 15:8–9).

You know that feeling when you have lost something that really is important to you? The woman in the Bible had ten valuable coins, but one was missing. She knew it had to be in the house, so she started sweeping everywhere, hoping it would turn up. When she swept under a table, her broom brought out the lost coin. She was thrilled, so thrilled that she called her friends and family to tell them the lost coin had been found. "Come celebrate with me! I found my lost coin!"

Although we are happy for this woman, this story doesn't seem that important for God to put it in His Word. Or is it? We need to study it.

There were ten coins, and one rolled out of sight. Not giving a thought to the other nine, a search started for that one missing coin.

That coin had no idea it was lost. It had no idea it was found, either. It is just a coin. What is God telling us? How does this relate to children and parents?

Ten Valuable Children

Look at it this way: Each bright, sparkling coin could represent a happy, bright-eyed child. Children are loved by God, talked about by God, lifted up by God, and protected by God. They are not aware of the worries of the world and are really just concerned with being happy and at play.

God sees children as shiny, bright delights, and He wants that none of them get out of His sight or away from His plans for their lives. Should that happen, though, just as the coin rolled off the table and was lost, the search is on. That valuable, happy, bright sparkle of a child is absolutely valuable to God—and to loving parents, as well. When the child is found, family and friends are called to rejoice in relief.

At that point, the child doesn't know about a divine plan for her or his life, doesn't even consider that others may be upset over that great hiding place she or he found, but wow, God does. God knows the purpose for which that child was created. In biblical terms, children God says are found means that He knows them to have accepted Jesus as their personal Savior, and now they have eternal life.

As with the woman and the lost coin, a child is going to be sought after until she or he has an understanding about Jesus, and until the child has professed that Jesus is Lord and is her or his personal Savior. When that happens, the child is labeled found.

Let's continue to read in Luke 15 where we left off:

"In the same way, I tell you, there is rejoicing in the presence of the angels of God over one sinner who repents" (Luke 15:10 NIV).

The Bible says that all the angels rejoice every time a lost soul turns to Jesus.

I firmly believe this is why God wants us to know this story. Now I know why God dedicated a whole chapter to the lost coin story found in these three verses of Luke.

Last week, Kendall, age eight, had an opportunity to lead a classmate to the Lord. I asked Kendall to tell me the story again so I could tell you. Here are her words that I wrote down as she told her story:

"Well, it all started when we were talking about something, and the boy at my table said, 'Oh, my [Kendall hesitated, not wanting to use God's name in vain, even telling me what another had said, but then she went on] God.'

"Another boy sitting at the table said to the boy, 'That's a bad word.'

"The first boy said, 'No, it's not.'

"'Yes, it is if you are a Christian,' the other boy told him, 'because we don't use God's name in an unimportant way. The way you used God was in an unimportant way.'

"The first boy asked, 'How do I become a Christian?'"

Kendall said, "So, I told him to pray after me, and he asked Jesus into his life."

Kendall and her tablemates were third graders, and we need to take their example. How often have we heard someone use God's name in vain? Maybe we cringe or just let it go altogether. But how simple it was that this child corrected his friend with gentleness. How easily it came about. A boy now has eternal life because his friend and Kendall were partnering with God.

Yes, God is using our children and grandchildren in a mighty way, and we are just seeing the tip of the iceberg of His plan with children.

If you listen to stories told by many pastors today, you will learn they were called by God into the ministry before reaching their teenage years. Some preached their first sermons before the age of fifteen.

God has used children throughout history, recording their stories in the Bible. But from what God has been showing me, today's move reveals a bigger plan, a plan that involves children moving in the supernatural realm as their daily norm. The things we will be learning from them as they pray and move mountains is so exciting.

Chapter 7

Why Did God Speak of These? Weeds/Wheat and Good Fish/Bad Fish

Carlisle took one look at the title for this chapter and right away understood the meaning and direction of God's comparing weeds with wheat plus the good fish with bad fish: all types of plants, all types of fish, all types of people.

We grow up with people, and we meet all types of people. If I don't stay true to my faith, I can be pulled in the wrong direction. We are all growing up together, so I really have to pay attention to the choices I make. Many people my age decide to go with choices I feel are wrong. It's hard not to be with that group. How do we know what to do? We need to start by looking at it from God's perspective as we think of what to do. By staying in the Bible and reading His Word, the Holy Spirit can remind us how gentle and right God is. By spending time with God, we begin to get how He thinks.

If I start to go the wrong way, I feel guilty. At first, I may think that I am getting away with something, but I feel so guilty that I stop and think. God always has people He can work through to help you turn to the right choice. There is always a way out. God can work through anyone, just anyone.

Look at this story from the book of Numbers about a donkey, an angel, and a prophet.

"Balaam got up in the morning, saddled his donkey and went with the Moabite officials. But God was very angry when he went, and the angel of the Lord stood in the road to oppose him. Balaam was riding on his donkey, and his two servants were with him. When the donkey saw the angel of the Lord standing in the road with a drawn sword in his hand, it turned off the road into a field. Balaam beat it to get it back on the road.

"Then the angel of the Lord stood in a narrow path through the vineyards, with walls on both sides. When the donkey saw the angel of the Lord, it pressed close to the wall, crushing Balaam's foot against it. So he beat the donkey again.

"Then the angel of the Lord moved on ahead and stood in a narrow place where there was no room to turn, either to the right or to the left. When the donkey saw the angel of the Lord, it lay down under Balaam, and he was angry and beat it with his staff. Then the Lord opened the donkey's mouth, and it said to Balaam, 'What have I done to you to make you beat me these three times?'

"Balaam answered the donkey, 'You have made a fool of me! If only I had a sword in my hand, I would kill you right now.'

"The donkey said to Balaam, 'Am I not your own donkey, which you have always ridden, to this day? Have I been in the habit of doing this to you?'

"'No,' he said.

"Then the Lord opened Balaam's eyes, and he saw the angel of the Lord standing in the road with his sword drawn. So he bowed low and fell facedown.

"The angel of the Lord asked him, 'Why have you beaten your donkey these three times? I have come here to oppose you because your path is a reckless one before me. The donkey saw me and turned away from me these three times. If it had not turned away, I would certainly have killed you by now, but I would have spared it.'

"Balaam said to the angel of the Lord, 'I have sinned. I did not realize you were standing in the road to oppose me. Now if you are displeased, I will go back.'

"The angel of the Lord said to Balaam, 'Go with the men, but speak only what I tell you.' So Balaam went with Balak's officials" (Numbers 22:21–35 NIV).

 In school, we learned from these verses that when we are faced with an issue, it is best to freeze and listen to God instead of doing things our own way. In this story, God was able to stop Balaam from getting killed by making the donkey freeze.

God will use whatever or whoever is around to get the attention of His people and show them what He needs them to do, like when God made a donkey talk just to get the attention of Balaam.

Sometimes at school, a group starts to be mean to someone, and I hate that. I wouldn't want to be the one being treated that way. I get beside them and become their friend, and we play together. If I see someone having a hard time, I quietly sit in class and pray for them. No one knows I'm doing that. I seem just normal, but that is what I do. Since I have always gone to Christian schools, people are not really mean there, but they have already formed a group of friends. A new person can feel sad and left out, so I watch out for them. That is what God would do.

Carlisle has just shared some mature thoughts. Let's take a closer look at what she has said.

Yes, children grow up together, and the good and the bad are all in the same school. It is hard to think of children as bad, but perhaps their parents haven't talked to them about making right choices, and these children crave attention. They get it with negative behavior. Some children are what we used to call latchkey kids. I heard a man say on TV today that he and his brother were latchkey kids. He said it was not a happy time, for his older brother had bipolar disorder, and he would often overpower him and beat him up. I certainly don't think that is the norm. I definitely hope that is not the normal situation for a child. Do they still call children who have to let themselves into an empty house latchkey kids?

No, I guess not because when I asked her, Carlisle had no idea what a latchkey kid was. I'll tell you. Their parents work, and some children have to let themselves into an empty house after school. They then give their parent a call to let them know they are safely home. Usually, there is a treat for them to eat as they do their homework. I have no idea who coined the term *latchkey children*, but that is what they were called then. This is not the case, normally, in a Christian school, but it is very much so in many public schools. Thankfully, I was never a latchkey kid. My mother was always there when I got home from school, as Jessica is for our granddaughters. That's a blessing from God. For those parents who both work, there are wonderful after-school care options they can choose from to make sure their children are safe.

There are parallels in the story of the weeds and the wheat. They grew up together in the same field, and when it came time for harvest, they were both pulled out at the same time, but each was put in a different pile—the one to which they belonged:

"Jesus told them another parable: 'The kingdom of heaven is like a man who sowed good seed in his field. But while everyone was sleeping, his enemy came and sowed weeds among the wheat, and went away. When the wheat sprouted and formed heads, then the weeds also appeared.

"'The owner's servants came to him and said, "Sir, didn't you sow good seed in your field? Where then did the weeds come from?"

"'"An enemy did this," he replied.

"'The servants asked him, "Do you want us to go and pull them up?"

"'"No," he answered, "because while you are pulling the weeds, you may uproot the wheat with them. Let both grow together until the harvest. At that time I will tell the harvesters: First collect the weeds and tie them in bundles to be burned; then gather the wheat and bring it into my barn"'" (Matthew 13:24–30 NIV).

I think of the final harvest of souls.

The parable of the wheat and weeds illustrates to us that, at the final harvest of souls, God will sort the good people from the bad people. He will throw bad people out and bless the good. I, for sure, would like to be in the blessed pile. With Jesus as my personal Savior, I am.

I know that God wants to bless all of us, but some have so hardened their hearts that it no longer seems possible. However, with God, all things are possible, so we need to pray for these people. Think about the biblical example of Saul, whose name was later changed to Paul. We can read all about this in Acts 9. Here is proof

that hearts can be changed when God is at work.

Weeds and wheat aren't mean and rude to each other like people can be, but the weeds grow and choke out the good wheat.

The Story of the Fish Net

What is the parable of the good fish and bad fish? They all climbed in the same net together. Well, maybe they didn't climb, but they were in the same spot as the net was let down. The net captured everything that was in its path. Could be good fish, bad fish, shoes, seaweed, whatever was in the path was caught as the net was closing.

"'Once again, the kingdom of heaven is like a net that was let down into the lake and caught all kinds of fish. When it was full, the fishermen pulled it up on the shore. Then they sat down and collected the good fish in baskets, but threw the bad away. This is how it will be at the end of the age. The angels will come and separate the wicked from the righteous and throw them into the blazing furnace, where there will be weeping and gnashing of teeth.

"'Have you understood all these things?' Jesus asked.

"'Yes,' they replied.

"He said to them, 'Therefore every teacher of the law who has become a disciple in the kingdom of heaven is like the owner of a house who brings out of his storeroom new treasures as well as old'" (Matthew 13:47–52 NIV).

What is Jesus telling us in this parable? We never know who around us is a target of Satan. We could be the target, but the others got caught too. Do you see what I am getting at? The trap Satan drops captures all in its path, and all are pulled up together.

Nevertheless, God is watching, and He sends the fishermen to separate the good fish from the bad fish. The net is pulled up, and then the good fish are carefully separated, and the bad fish are destroyed.

In the case of the weeds and the corn, the farmer pulls them up together and then carefully separates his harvest from the weeds that tried to destroy it.

1 Corinthians 10:13 tells us that God will always provide a way to escape, to get us away from whatever is trying to destroy us. I've learned it's up to us to make the right choice to take that escape route. Here is that verse:

"No temptation has overtaken you except what is common to mankind. And God is faithful; he will not let you be tempted beyond what you can bear. But when you are tempted, he will also provide a way out so that you can endure it" (1 Corinthians 10:13 NIV).

The Holy Spirit is supernatural. Be sensitive to what the Holy Spirit inside of you is saying. Be accustomed to hearing His still small voice, on the receiving end, and He will direct your path. This helps you from getting tangled with the weeds or the bad fish.

He will keep your natural spirit, which is not supernatural, from following the crowd, so to speak, and ending up in trouble.

There is a real problem now with the forces that are at work in the world. It's the weed or bad fish that prevents people from thinking accurately. Those who followed the wrong crowd have become perverted by the enemy. In other words, the enemy has made them wicked and sinful. They do things that are so hateful, so evil, and they are destroying innocent lives. This is why it is so important to be influenced by the Holy Spirit and be alert to His leading us, for it will be away from the enemy's traps.

Christian culture is the only thing that guarantees freedom, and the enemy is trying to push back against those who have Jesus as their personal Savior. We continue pushing ahead with our strong faith, and the enemy hates that. This is what he does. The enemy gets us really busy, just no time to read the scriptures or pray, for we are just busy. Or does he have you worried? If you are worried, your focus is on the problem, not the answer. Let go of it, and give it to God; that's the answer. God has to stop working if you take it back. God tells us to cast our cares upon Him, for He cares for you. That's in 1 Peter 5:7. We need to obey this verse. If Jesus is our personal Savior, then Jesus tells us to give Him our concerns and stop worrying about them.

Depression. Depression is another tactic of separating a Christian from relying on God and reading the Bible. It's an oppression of heaviness over a person, making it hard to pray or read the Bible. A depressed person loses all hope.

Disease. Disease is not from God. Being worried and depressed can make a person sick.

Delight in the Lord. God is so interested in each one of us. Psalm 24:1 tells us, "The earth is the Lord's, and everything in it." God made all different kinds of fruit, for example, so that all of us children would not miss out on being able to have something we like that is good for us.

Psalm 37:4 says, "Take delight in the Lord, and He will give you the desires of your heart." He will meet our needs and grant us the desires of our heart, for our hearts and desires will start matching what He wanted for us all along. God truly knows what will make us the happiest. He knows us better than we know ourselves.

The supernatural Holy Spirit is inside everyone who has accepted Christ as their personal Savior. Being alert to the Holy Spirit is the key to a blessed life. That's our answer. The Holy Spirit in us wants to guide us and keep us out of Satan's traps. God would love that the evil people in this world would come to know Him, not to be sorted out and destroyed, as are the weeds and the bad fish.

"'Do I have any pleasure in the death of the wicked,' declares the Lord GOD, 'rather than that he should turn from his ways and live'" (Ezekiel 18:23).

"'For I have no pleasure in the death of anyone who dies,' declares the Lord GOD. 'Therefore, repent and live'" (Ezekiel 18:32).

God wants all people to be saved and to come to a knowledge of the truth. 1 Timothy 2:4 tells us that. God wants us to have peace in this world.

We've learned a lot here. Every time you see a weed, think of the Holy Spirit wanting to show you the right way to go. The weed will remind you that the road the Holy Spirit leads you on is a smooth highway, away from the enemy's traps. Staying tuned into Him is what we must do. How many times has He whispered something to you, you hear Him, but carry on your way, very soon finding there was a reason to obey what you heard? I do that, realize I'm on the wrong path, and remember my quiet warning I had received. How often have I had to say to God, "Will I ever learn to heed your warnings?"

Chapter 8

I Hear You Knocking

> Here I am! I stand at the door and knock. If anyone
> hears my voice and opens the door, I will come in
> and eat with that person, and they with me.
> —Revelation 3:20 (NIV)

I learned this verse as a little girl, and it remains my favorite. I have special memories of visiting with Jesus because of this verse. Before going to sleep at night, I opened the door of my heart and let Jesus in. I visited with him, offering him something to drink (which He never accepted), and we just spent time together.

There is a door to your heart, but there is no knob on the outside. It is just on the inside, so you have to be the one to turn the knob and open the door. There He is, right outside that door, waiting. I didn't know that He only needed to be invited in once. I pretended to open that door every night so I could visit with Jesus. We actually do have to pray over and over. If we don't communicate daily with our Lord, we are ignoring Him. We have Jesus in our heart but are not talking with Him. We are being so rude.

Imagine that you invited a friend into your house but went about your day without a thought of your friend, as he or she just sat on the couch, watching you come and go. Jesus not only wants for us talk with Him, He also wants to talk to us. Each new day is a gift that He gives us. He wants to lead us, bless us, and set up divine connections, people we are supposed to meet. What a waste of a day if we are not led by God.

I was recently asked to write a guest blog on AnchoringHope. com. God had just dealt with me in an unusual way about ignoring Jesus, ignoring the Holy Spirit, and ignoring God. Let me share that story of mine. This is just a sample of my guest blog that appeared on their website:

It Never Entered My Mind

While driving along and listening to a radio station that plays songs from the 1940s, a Richard Rogers and Lorenz Hart song came on from one of their musicals. The title was "It Never Entered My Mind," and it was written one year before I was born. I can honestly say I have heard it all my life.

That song kept coming back to my mind throughout the day, and I finally just said out loud, "Heavenly Father, what is this all about? What do you want me to know?"

Well, I had asked God. Thoughts started coming. Could it be that I had not put Him anywhere in my life that day? Had I just had been off on my own? Was God telling me that He never entered my mind today?

Oh, I hope that's not it. I was just really busy today, and I can't believe God never entered my mind. Oh, heavenly Father, I'm so ashamed and so very sorry if that is the case. Please forgive me.

I had to be an easy target for the devil if that's the case. I was not even aware I was in his trap and in a spiritual battle. Apathetic. That is what I was—apathetic—if that was the reason for that song to keep playing in my head.

The definition of apathy is an absence of passion or emotion, a lack of interest or concern for things that others find moving or exciting

I must have been in a pitiful state that day. It is so hard to believe it didn't occur to me to get with God, nor did I give a thought about missing all that.

I was no worry to Satan, none at all. I for sure was not the light reflecting God, nor was I the salt of the earth. I was not aware I was trapped. How sad is that?

Satan tempts us all the time. We have three choices when tempted:

1) We can give in, not even try to fight it.
2) We can give up, give up on trying to resist it.
3) We can grow through it.

James 4:7 (NIV) tells us to "submit yourself to God then, resist the devil, and he will flee."

How do we do that, resist the devil? Be a reader of the Word. The truth of God is in the Bible and will keep us walking with the Lord on the straight path.

But wait a minute! I had read the Bible for almost an hour that day before I got in that apathetic state. What's up with that? I had started the day with God. What went wrong that I was confronted by a song that wouldn't stop playing?

Well, it is the difference between accumulating facts and applying truth, of giving orders to God about my day rather than delighting in the Lord and the joy of being in His presence. The difference of being under the influence of His wonderful mighty hand, rather than off into busyness again.

I had read the Word, closed the book, and didn't apply a thing I read. My heart must not have realized that my heavenly Father was so hurt to see me not even glance at Him as I checked off the box that said to pray and walked off to do my "important things." Thankfully, God called me out on that through a song on the radio that would keep hitting replay in my mind. Thankfully, I wasn't allowed to continue in the apathetic state I was in.

I humbled myself before the Lord, feeling chastened, embarrassed, ashamed, and very loved. God disciplines the ones He loves. Hebrews 12:6 tells us that. He treated me as a daughter with loving discipline.

Do you see how dangerous apathetic people are? We aren't walking in our blessings, we aren't being God's instruments to reach the lost, we are being robbed of our gift of that day, robbed of those blessings we could have had and the lives we could have touched.

I don't have to say any more. I know you are not in that apathetic state, for here you are, reading this blog of hope. Thankfully, you are alert to the voice of God. Thankfully, when temptation comes, you ask Jesus to answer the door.

Keep it up! Apply the Word of God and remain alert and alive in Christ.

I have found twenty-three verses on apathy and indifference to God. I can memorize them and fight back now.

Thank You, heavenly Father, for loving me so much that you used a song to shake me out of my apathetic state. May I stay alert to your voice and obedient to your directions. Please! In Jesus's name, Amen.

The original post about a conversation with God can be seen on AnchoringHope.com.

Indeed, it is such a loss when we are off on our own and not being led by the Lord. We are busy, and we think we are doing fine, until we realize what has been going on. Then we are terribly ashamed and sad, and we have to humble ourselves before our God and ask to be forgiven. Let's instead be faithful to be alert to His voice and obedient to His direction. Let's be as faithful as a child who just simply wants to visit with Him.

If apathy has been going on in your life, ask for forgiveness. There are days when I need to ask forgiveness, and I ask to be pulled back into His presence and be guided by Him. Indeed, it is a great loss when we are off on our own, without being led by the Lord.

That child who pictures Jesus with them, just spills out thoughts, and listens to what He has to say, can then peacefully go off to sleep. I know, for I grew up doing that.

That is why childlike faith is so pure. Things are simple, without thought. Before going off to sleep, it is fun to just picture Jesus and tell Him about your hopes and all that went on in the day. That is how it was with me.

Mature faith knows we need to start our day in prayer, asking Jesus to guide us as we start out in this gift of a new day. We should be in prayer throughout the day, and indeed we can end our day like that little child before peacefully going off to sleep. Oh, and be sure to tell Him what you are thankful for in your day's experience, and ask forgiveness for any sin you might have committed.

Let's see what Carlisle thinks about Revelation 3:20:

Open the Door of Your Heart

I know this verse means God is waiting at the door of your heart. When you open the door and ask Him in, He will come. Then I pray, or as I like to call it when I'm talking to Him, He listens. When I ask Him a question, even if I don't hear His voice, still the eyes of my heart are opened to the right choice. He answers my questions.

I think when you first become a Christian and ask Him into your heart, you want to make sure that God stays there, so the two of you can keep talking. So I asked Him in over and over again. I for sure want Him to stay there. I do know that God never leaves my side, and He is always there for me. This verse helps me remember that.

Realizing that Jesus is in your heart (for He is, if you asked Him in) enables you to make the best of each day. Bask in His great love that forgives sins and takes us into the family of God. Jesus Christ is powerful; even His name is powerful. Nothing can stand against the power of that name—Jesus Christ.

We've talked about this new day as a gift from God. We are to rejoice and be glad in it. We only get one chance to live this life, and it can be spent however we wish, but if spent giving glory to our heavenly Father and in our full potential, how wonderful. How wonderful that could be. The Lord is on your side; who can harm you? That is a promise in the Bible:

"I cried to the Lord in my trouble, and He answered me and put me in a good place. The Lord is with me. I will not be afraid of what man can do to me" (Psalm 118:5–6 NLV).

Picturing Jesus standing right in front of you lets your day be wonderfully connected to the source of all you need. Hanging around Jesus lets you become more and more like Him. Ask Him to help you live the plan He has for you this new day. Squeeze out every ounce of living in the presence of your Lord and Savior each day. Sound like a good idea? It is possible.

Don't worry about yesterday. We ended yesterday when we fell asleep. Don't worry about tomorrow. Jesus will be there to talk to tomorrow. God says His name is I AM. He lives in the present. He didn't say his name is I Was. God wants us to make this day He has given us the best it can be. He has fun surprises, rich blessings, amazing love, and protection for us today. Enjoy this day the Lord has made, and keep talking to our Lord as we go about it.

Set Your Priorities for Each Day

I have learned it is wonderful to set your priorities for your day, making God first. Spending time in the morning in this prayer time we have been talking about, reading out of the Bible, having breakfast and getting ready for the day, enjoying your family are all wonderful priorities. Decide your goal for the day, and even write it down. You will know what you have to do, so that will be easy. Commit to getting that done.

My goal this morning was to work on writing this chapter, and I have committed time to do it. It indeed is getting done, and I have peace as a result. A child may need to prepare for a test coming up.

Albert Einstein said if you want to live a happy life, tie it to a goal. I am saying that goal should be what God needs you to do today. I am also saying that goal should be becoming more and more like Him. Another goal is that your life bring glory to our heavenly Father. God created each of us for a purpose, and letting God lead you to it and through it is a wonderful goal. That requires staying in prayer with the one we opened the door to: Jesus Christ.

Chapter 9

Holy Spirit, Even Today, Teach Us

This was a unique chapter to write. The Holy Spirit indeed taught Carlisle and me as we wrote about Him. When we got together to work on this chapter, reading what the two of us had written as we both were working alone with the Lord, Carlisle and I found that both of us had been touched by His presence. We were so touched by the presence of the Holy Spirit that we both wept with joy. Carlisle and I were not together when that happened. Neither of us had told each other what had happened until putting this chapter together, and neither of us cry easily. The Holy Spirit is so kind, so full of love, and so wants the best for us. It just is sometimes quite emotional to realize you are having a conversation with the Spirit of the Lord. I just wanted to share that with you. You may feel His presence strongly.

What the Holy Spirit wants is for that relationship to be normal, for us to talk with the Holy Spirit throughout each and every day. God wants us to tap into the supernatural power of the Holy Spirit. Yes, it is real, and yes, you know when you are talking to Him. That's why the apostle Paul so earnestly wanted everyone he mentored to experience the fellowship of the Holy Spirit.

"May the grace of the Lord Jesus Christ, and the love of God, and the fellowship of the Holy Spirit be with you all" (2 Corinthians 13:14 NIV).

Why doesn't everyone want this?

I was remembering reading what Carlisle had written about all she knew about the Holy Spirit before this encounter.

As a matter of fact, I'll let you read it:

The Holy Spirit makes you feel guilty when you're bad. He doesn't want a sin to separate you from God. He is like God's gift to us when we accept Jesus into our hearts. I do know that about the Holy Spirit. The Holy Spirit can fill us up and whisper what is right and what is wrong.

My question is, where can I learn more about the Holy Spirit? I don't exactly have a question, because I know close to nothing about this incredible gift God has put in me. I want to learn so much about the Holy Spirit and everything else about God's creation and His Word. I want to learn so much that I guess my question would be, "How could I know all this, and how can I share this with people?"

I asked the Holy Spirit this question: "Just how do I go about teaching our grandchildren about You?" Then I got busy doing something else, but the Holy Spirit for sure wanted me to know the answer.

The next morning, I was doing my Bible study, and as I turned the pages, they seemed to be stuck by a tiny spot in each corner. I finished my study, separating the pages as I turned, but instead of closing my Bible, I continued through to the back, wondering how many more pages were suddenly stuck at the corners. I was on 3 John, so there weren't that many more pages.

I kept telling myself that this was not necessary; I could separate the pages as I came to them tomorrow. Nevertheless, I persevered in my self-imposed job, past Jude, past Revelation, to a section in the back I had never noticed before. There it was, all written out for me: the answer to my question about teaching about the Holy Spirit.

This is what I learned: If you want to teach about the Holy Spirit, simply do this. Ask them to write down a question that they have for God. That's it, nothing more. Don't ask to see it.

The Holy Spirit teaches about Himself, and we are never to try to do the job of the Holy Spirit. The next morning, I heard the same thing I had read in that Bible resource as I was listening to a Christian channel on TV.

So in the morning, He showed me the answer in the Bible, and a day later followed up with speaking through a minister on TV. That minister was telling us that a person should never think about doing the work of the Holy Spirit. I had my answer, and I believe you do, as well.

The next morning, I was on a webinar, and I shared what I just told you with the others. James, also on the webinar from Illinois, reminded us that God thinks, Jesus speaks, and the Holy Spirit acts.

Think about it. It was the Holy Spirit who hovered over the waters when God said, "Let there be light." There was light, and God said it was good. If the Holy Spirit can make light, there is not a doubt in my mind that He can reveal Himself to our young grandchildren.

"Now the earth was formless and empty, darkness was over the surface of the deep, and the Spirit of God was hovering over the waters. And God said, 'Let there be light,' and there was light. God saw that the light was good, and he separated the light from the darkness" (Genesis 1:2–4 NIV).

When I was a little girl, the Holy Spirit used to give me the peace that passes all understanding. I could just ask for it, and that amazing feeling of indescribable peace would be all over me. I then always asked for Him to give it to my dad or my mother, for I wanted them to feel it, as well. They didn't know I did that, and I never knew if they were aware. They were downstairs, and I was upstairs in my room, visiting with God.

As a child, it was wonderful to just ask for that peaceful feeling and receive it. As an adult, I have to focus on God and be aware of what is going on and how God moved in my situation, and usually when thanking God, that peace overwhelms me. Or sometimes even during my actions or words in a certain situation, the Holy Spirit will suddenly pour that peace all over me. It lets me know that He is aware and watching and says, "Way to go, girl!" Those times are special.

Make It a Goal to Hear from God Each Day

Want to know how to hear from God each day? Let that be one of your goals for the day. I make it a daily goal, writing down under Goals: Hear from God. He surely loves to talk with you.

I write down the goals that I want to reach every day. Goals have to be written down. I don't know why, but there is something that happens when you write them down. I can't explain it; just do it, and see for yourself.

That being one of your goals—to hear from God—your focus is on God in each and everything that goes on in the day. You suddenly realize you are hearing from Him. You realize it and say, "Hey, that is God working in this situation."

I journal how I've heard from Him each day. I might hear through the Bible, through another person, or via a still small voice or a quick thought.

Yesterday, I had been praying about how I could pay off an unexpected dental bill. Then, I learned at the oral surgeon's office that I might possibly need more dental work. I was there seeing if an implant could have a crown placed over it. The x-ray taken for that showed something on another tooth. That's so not what I wanted to hear. I don't like owing anything on a credit card, and I choose to pay my own dental bills. Insurance was used up, and this new problem would be all mine. My dentist sent me to a specialist. A powerful two-dimensional x-ray showed a possible fracture and, at best, a problem that needed retreatment on the root of that tooth. Retreatment would be about $1,000, but a fracture would mean another extraction and another implant, plus a new crown to replace the crown already there. With insurance already used up for the year, that would be another bunch of money.

Nothing in my mouth was hurting, but if this had to be done, my bank account would certainly hurt. I don't like to make Bob pay for my dental work, especially since we had an unexpected foundation problem at this same time. I took this on myself. Unfortunately, my generation was already in their teens when fluoride came out. Therefore, we don't have the strong cavity-free healthy teeth the generations following us had. I so wish we did, for fillings over the years eventually caused teeth to need root canals, and now decades later, many of us are needing those teeth extracted and implants put in. I don't know why, nor did I expect this ever to happen. You have no idea how I wish we had fluoride before I was thirteen. I had actually enjoyed four cleaning visits with no problems found, but suddenly things seemed to have changed. Surprises like that after a dental checkup are very unwelcome.

I got a call from my regular dentist. The receptionist told me that she needed to see me before my next appointment with the specialist, as she had gotten his report for the consult. I was in a bookstore near her office anyway, so I dropped by the dentist's office.

Because I was not having any symptoms, she advised me to just monitor the tooth rather than undergo treatment, since what they saw on the x-ray my dentist had already been watching for five years, and it seemed to have resolved itself.

The key point here is my dentist approached me. I had not talked to her about what the specialist had said, nor was I aware she even knew of my upcoming appointment. I knew that I had heard from God through another person, my dentist. Her recommendation would save me several thousand dollars. I felt like a mountain had been lifted from my shoulders. I told her that her advice was an answer to prayer.

I just used the example of this unexpected dental expense, but you may have had an unexpected house expense or medical expense. We had that too: an unexpected house expense at the same time that was far more involved than the dental work. You can use the same principle I am going to tell you about. There is a reason I am boring you with my dental experience. Of course, Bob was handling the house expense. I do have a point I want to make.

Sometimes, There is a "However," But Hang On

However, later that same day, I got a call from my dentist's receptionist again, saying that my dentist had talked to the endodontist to be sure it was all right to just monitor the tooth for a while. She explained that what they were seeing, she had seen five years ago, and her thinking was it had resolved by itself. He explained more of what he was thinking, and she wanted to discuss it with me. I was given a consult appointment for eleven o'clock the next day.

I'll tell you that it seemed I went from cloud nine to the bottom of a roller coaster. I told God that I thought I had heard from Him, and I had been so very thankful and happy.

"You know, Lord, that would be so much more money to have to pay right now, as I'm paying for the tooth that was worked on last month, plus the publishing costs for this book. Another three thousand dollars or more is just too much."

God had a surprise for me.

When I woke up the next morning, I dreaded that appointment. I asked the Holy Spirit to go with me, for I could not go alone.

I didn't know that God had a surprise for me.

It turned out that my dentist's recommendation to continue monitoring my tooth was still the best option, so I was saving the $3,000 the dental work was estimated to cost.

Later that day, as I drove home from a hair appointment, I was remembering all I had to be thankful for that day. Suddenly, there He was: the Holy Spirit.

I said, "Hi, Holy Spirit! Thank you so much for all that you did for me today, for I had some worries about how that consult appointment was going to turn out."

As I was talking to the Holy Spirit, I realized tears were flowing. I guess I was just so relieved, so very happy.

How did I know the Holy Spirit was suddenly there? It's like a friend coming up behind you and tapping you on the shoulder. I just felt a warmth, a peace, and I knew immediately it was the Holy Spirit.

Our daughter owns IHN Media Services, a national media advertising business. About the same time the dental decisions were in the forefront, she texted that she had the potential for a really wonderful client who wanted to advertise with her. She asked that I pray for this. I told her I already had and sent her my prayer list. The second thing on the list was: "Please send Susie a magnificent client." She was amazed.

There was to be a conference call the next morning so Susan could go over the proposal, but the client didn't answer the phone. Knowing the roller-coaster ride I had just been on with my faith, I told her it was going to be fine.

Indeed, it was, for two days later, she was told she had the contract. However, that roller coaster plummeted downward again. The next meeting that was to take place hadn't yet happened; the contract hadn't been signed, nor had money been exchanged.

I told her that she needed to ask the Holy Spirit what she should know about this. Susan said she would. She really liked this company and the people in it, and was looking forward to working with them. I did as well, and I was happy they had chosen her to help them with their advertising. I suddenly remembered the verse in the Bible that says not to worry:

"Give thanks in all circumstances; for this is God's will for you in Christ Jesus" (1 Thessalonians 5:18 NIV)

Later that day, I asked Susan what she had heard. She felt that He told her to relax. Putting the two together, she said, "I guess I'm not to worry and relax."

I have told several people going through things that if you believe you truly have heard from the Holy Spirit, to hold onto what it is you believe, even if it means going on a roller-coaster ride. While praying this evening about that contract, and believing that her client indeed was from the Lord, I was stopped right there and flooded with that peace that passes all understanding.

Philippians 4:7 is where that reference is found: "And the peace of God, which transcends all understanding, will guard your hearts and your minds in Christ Jesus."

Hold onto your faith when you have a knowing that you have heard from the Holy Spirit. Even in these two instances, when it looked like we had heard wrong, what we were told by the Holy Spirit was actually the result. Even though down I went on the emotional roller-coaster ride again, I kept getting confirmation. That's actually three confirmations that I received and therefore very solid advice.

Every born-again Christian has the gift of the Holy Spirit. Jesus spoke of this.

Jesus Promises the Holy Spirit

"If you love me, keep my commands. And I will ask the Father, and he will give you another advocate to help you and be with you forever" (John 14:15–16 NIV).

The Work of the Holy Spirit

"When the Advocate comes, whom I will send to you from the Father—the Spirit of truth who goes out from the Father—he will testify about me" (John 15:26 NIV).

"But when he, the Spirit of truth, comes, he will guide you into all the truth. He will not speak on his own; he will speak only what he hears, and he will tell you what is yet to come" (John 16:13 NIV).

The Holy Spirit is our comforter, our intercessor. He stands by us and strengthens us. We have the perfect counselor inside us, wanting to influence us so our steps are sure and right. Let's help our children get acquainted with Him. He has a rich and full supply of provisions for us.

The key to tapping into His provisions is spending time with the Holy Spirit inside of you. Seek His counsel, enjoy being with Him, and watch the Holy Spirit work for your best interests.

If there is a choice of things to do, and something seems better to our natural spirit, our natural spirit would lead us that way.

The Holy Spirit is supernatural and knows secrets about what the one choice that doesn't seem better would offer. He will lead us the better way.

We want to make the right choice, and Carlisle said she knows the Holy Spirit will let us know which one that is. I think Carlisle just wanted to know how that answer comes, but as she wrote this book, the presence of the Holy Spirit manifested in a beautiful way. She'll be sharing more as you keep reading.

The answer to the question she had written down for the Holy Spirit, and how the answer would come, were both revealed as we worked on this chapter. At the time, Carlisle couldn't help but cry with the emotion she could still feel, and since I wasn't there, she wanted to tell me the whole story. The emotion of just telling the story to me brought her back to tears of joy. She was so full of emotion that she couldn't sit still and barely could write. She did, though. Let's read her words:

 I had asked the Holy Spirit if my life would have an impact on the world. But as time went on, I wasn't thinking about that question much anymore. One day, Caitlin and I were talking, and I told her about stuff like changing the world for God. I told her that

there were forces out to get Christians, and this was all real. At this time, Caitlin was having a doubt all kids have at this age, which is really scary. She thought she wasn't going to go to heaven. I had prayed a lot for God to give me the right words to help her. I had tried on my own, for she had told me this before, but it obviously all failed. Then, I had a sister meeting in the little alcove under the stairs. There, I told them all I've just told you at the beginning of this paragraph. Kendall didn't exactly connect or understand this like Caitlin did, so she left. Then Caitlin was brave enough to tell me about her dream. In the dream, she was reading the Bible with her friends, and when she closed the Bible, her friend said, "Wait, I want to read more." After her friend said that in the dream, Caitlin woke up and started crying. It's hard to understand why her friend saying that would cause so much emotion, but the sheer power of the dream woke her up so full of emotion that she was crying After Caitlin told me this, the Holy Spirit gave me the words to say. I don't really remember all I told her, but now I was in tears, and so was she. Then after what seemed like a long time, she wasn't afraid anymore. We went to my mom. Mom thought I had done something to Caitlin, since she could see she had been crying. Caitlin assured her I hadn't done anything to her, and then we told Mom all that had happened.

The annoying thing about grown-ups is, it's hard for them to understand this kind of stuff and grasp the full power of it. I don't know why that is. Anyway, Mom took us to the bathroom to clean us up because we had tears streaming down our faces. We literally could not stop bawling for half an hour. It was hard to tell Mom all I told Caitlin. Finally, Caitlin said to me through her tears, "You have to talk really fast before you start crying again." Then she turned to Mom and said, "Mommy, I truly believe Carli is going to help change the world one day."

I suddenly realized God had answered my question, and it didn't come from some prophetic dream or holy acquaintance. It came from a crying little girl, changed by God. So now I know God is going to use me to help change the world.

Well, you can imagine both girls in tears, tears of nothing but joy. The Holy Spirit must have been so present with them in the room that the emotion couldn't be stopped. Remember, they couldn't really explain it to their mother, so Carlisle wasn't sure at this point that her mom understood what had just happened. If you are a grown-up, and you are having trouble grasping the impact of this, Carlisle has you in "the trouble with grown-ups" category.

"For those who are led by the Spirit of God are the children of God" (Romans 8:14 NIV).

All of us who have accepted Jesus as our personal Savior have the Holy Spirit present in us. God has something bigger for each of us than our human minds can imagine—something eternal. God knows everything about us, and we need to submit to Him. We need to tap into the Holy Spirit.

The Greek word for *submit* means to put in order, to be under. God is so holy and so worthy of our wanting to be with Him, so let's learn to submit ourselves to Him. He wants only the best for us, so let's submit to God.

When God tells you to do something, it is for a good reason, and He knows you can do it.

Quality time in prayer is key; the rest just follows. Seek first the kingdom of God, and God will feed you. He feeds the birds and looks after the flowers of the field. You are more important. Train yourself to automatically go to God in prayer as quickly as you automatically bring your hand back when touching a hot stove. It should be an automatic reflex to pray, to bring God into the situation from the start. Prayer is not supposed to be the last resort.

We Are Waiting for the Spectacular and Missing the Supernatural

The secret of getting into your destiny is a real quality time of prayer. Are you stuck? Remember, Israel got to walk across the Red Sea on dry ground. You won't be stuck; the Red Sea will open for you too. God looks out for our ultimate good. Submit to Him.

Did you get in trouble? If you get in trouble with the Lord, talk to Him about it. He knows when your motive is right. If you messed up, submit to God—the God of grace and forgiveness.

We are waiting for the spectacular and therefore missing the supernatural. Celebrate the small beginnings with praise. You don't have to wait for the manifestation of the full result to thank God. Wonders of the world start with small beginnings.

God is trying to let us know how He is moving, and I shared what the Holy Spirit inspired me to write in each chapter of my first book. Amos 3:7 tells us that God lets us know His plans ahead of time:

"Surely the Sovereign LORD does nothing without revealing his plan to his servants the prophets" (Amos 3:7 NIV).

That is what *Restore, Restore, Restore and More* is all about. God said it is time for us to know these things, that yes, He is moving, and that the amazing restorations that we are starting to see will increase.

God allowed me through the Spirit of the Lord to write about His plans and agenda, and that book became a number one bestseller after two days. That was God's doing, not mine. He wants us to be alert to what He is working on so we can join Him. God wants us to be prepared and put our feet in action to join Him.

Even though I am a teacher, I can't teach chemistry in school. I don't know chemistry. I can teach multiplication, division, comprehension, and sentence diagramming, for I know how to do all of those. I think there is not a lot of teaching about the Holy

Spirit because people really don't have a grasp about Him and what He does.

Carlisle said it best. I guess my question would be, "How could I know all this, and how can I share this with people?"

"The human spirit is the lamp of the Lord that sheds light on one's inmost being" (Proverbs 20:27 NIV).

The Holy Spirit doesn't guide through our physical senses but through our heart, your innermost part, your belly. That is the source of the saying, "Go with your gut feeling."

You can't just feel what His leading is. The Holy Spirit doesn't guide through our physical senses. He is a candle, searching you and knowing your innermost thoughts. He looks at your spirit, not your body. He guides your spirit. We are made in the likeness of God, so we are a spirit being.

When our body is dead, yet we live. Our spirit lives on. Our spirit isn't dead.

Once again, the Holy Spirit speaks to our inner spirit and we sense it in our heart. Our heart is now after the same thing God wants, and what's in our hearts, we act on. It's wonderful to act on what God thought, what He shared that He wants us to do in a certain situation. Be alert to that inner witness. Remember, the inner witness—the Holy Spirit—is supernatural. Be alert, in tune with His guidance.

You may be looking for a job or a house. You walk into one place, and it is as if a buzzer goes off in your insides. Your head is thinking one thing, your heart another, but you don't want to miss the Holy Spirit's leading—His inward witness. This happened to me when we moved from Chicago to Dallas over twelve years ago. We had looked at many houses, and Bob was working with the builder on the contract for the one we chose. It was a gorgeous new home, and we both liked it, but as I sat there, I suddenly had no peace about that house. We had also looked at another house in this same neighborhood, and as I thought about that one, I had a real peace about it. We went with the one I had that real peace about, and we have been so happy with this one. I don't know what the difference would have been. I do know there was a very real lack of peace about the other one, and I do know that we are very happy in this one.

We follow the inward witness. Our inner self has a voice, a conscience, or maybe we could call it an intuition. If we have accepted Christ, old things have passed away, and all become new (2 Corinthians 5:17). That means the conscience and intuition are new. Therefore, it is safe to follow them.

If we are not followers of Christ, our inward self will let us do anything, fall into any trap. Our unsaved inward self is not safe.

The Holy Spirit is living inside the born-again Christian, and He doesn't communicate with your mind. He communicates in your spirit; therefore, our heart is safe.

We are in a covenant where God put His law in our inward parts. What are your inward parts?

"May God himself, the God of peace, sanctify you through and through. May your whole spirit, soul and body be kept blameless at the coming of our Lord Jesus Christ" (1 Thessalonians 5:23 NIV).

"On the last and greatest day of the festival, Jesus stood and said in a loud voice, 'Let anyone who is thirsty come to me and drink. Whoever believes in me, as Scripture has said, rivers of living water will flow from within them.' By this he meant the Spirit, whom those who believed in him were later to receive. Up to that time the Spirit had not been given, since Jesus had not yet been glorified" (John 7:37–39 NIV).

You can tell when you are led by the flesh or led by the Holy Spirit.

When someone hits you, your flesh just wants to hit them back. However, your Holy Spirit-led spirit pays no attention to any wrong done to you. Your spirit, led by the Holy Spirit, will rejoice when things are right and true, yet will bear up under anything.

The Holy Spirit-led spirit looks for the best in every person. What a nice quality.

The Holy Spirit is the love of God, the power of God, and the heart of God. God's love needs to be spread abroad, as the Spirit loves others through you.

The Holy Spirit living in your spirit isn't talking to your mind but to your spirit. You are a temple of God with the Holy Spirit inside of you. With Him inside of you, He will speak to your heart, which influences your mind.

Listen to your heart. It won't let you crash without a check (a warning) in your spirit. Throughout the years, I often admitted, "You told me, Holy Spirit. If only I had listened to You."

Your flesh can and sometimes will ignore your spirit. Believe God, and be alert to what He says to do. I have sometimes found myself in a mess when not paying attention to what was right and true. When I think about it, I can't deny the fact that I had a clear, quiet warning not to take that step. I ignored it, and I had consequences that were not fun.

Holy Spirit, even today, teach us just how to pray. Teach us to listen to those warnings and not find out the hard way why we should have done so. Holy Spirit, I love you. Teach us how to love through You. Help us to spread the love of God around.

Chapter 10

Prayer versus Intercession: Aren't They the Same?

Having spent hours with the Holy Spirit yesterday, working on His chapter, I immediately put this question to Him: What is the difference between prayer and intercession?

Carlisle and I had not even talked about this, but as I read what she had written, and having heard what the Holy Spirit told me, she nailed it. She has a strong grip on the difference and has experienced both. Prepare to be enlightened:

I think that people think they are praying when they are actually interceding.

Seriously, when was the last time you had a *real* conversation with God? I mean, when you just sat there and told Him your thoughts. Mostly we just "pray" to God about ourselves or for others. So, technically, we are interceding.

Praying is talking to God, just having a time where you are figuring things out about yourself and the world around you.

I'm not a pro at this. Truly, I've only prayed the kind of prayer I'm trying to tell you about three times. And let me tell you that when I did, I started crying. I was so overwhelmed by joy, and also a big feeling of peace and safety came over me.

I had just started making it a practice to read the Bible each day. Most people don't think of Genesis as a very spiritual book that will teach you life lessons, ones that you'll remember forever. But, when reading, it was like I felt the true joy of knowing God. Words can't explain it; it is amazing. As I said, you feel at peace and loved, safe, and overwhelmingly happy.

Interceding isn't bad at all. It is how most people talk to God. It is more just going through a list of the things you need or your family needs. You may also have a list of friends who need help from God. Certainly, praying for them is not bad, but there is a difference between a personal prayer relationship with God and praying for the needs of others. Do you see that?

Those are wonderful thoughts, and Carlisle explained it to us so well.

Notes from My Journal

I had also asked this question: "Holy Spirit, what is the difference between prayer and intercession? Is there a difference?" This is what I sensed He wanted me to know, and I journaled as fast as the thoughts came.

Intercession is a gift, one that can be used mightily. Intercession requires time, love, and compassion. Things may look hopeless, but the intercessor never doubts, knowing that God is able to work all things together for good (Romans 8:28). The intercessor's prayers continue. Even when time seems to have run out, the intercessor still comes with that prayer of faith. It is easy to recognize a true gifted intercessor.

Prayer is exactly what Carlisle said. It is a beautiful time, talking with the Lord, laughing with the Lord, and learning from the Lord. He is there to just let you pour out your heart. He never turns away and never thinks about something else or just pretends to listen. He is there. He loves you and wants you to do just what you are doing: pouring your heart out to Him.

Just Some Thoughts

I bet that He enjoys looking into the eyes of His children as they pray. Do you think so? The eyes are the window of the soul.

You are unique, and He knows all that made you unique. He knows the trials, the goals you've set, the desires you have, the love, the compassion, the joys—all you've been through that formed your uniqueness. He loves all that about you.

I wonder. I wonder if God saves special prayers of His children in a book to remember our love for Him. It could be like a Father's Day gift to Him that you offered every day.

Thinking about all these things gave me peace. They gave me such hope that all my prayers for my family, for the people I've met through these books I've written, and for the prayers I've prayed for myself have all been heard. We know God hears us, so just enjoy God while He is at work on your prayers. God knows the motives behind those prayers, remember, so make sure you have prayed for the right reason.

Sometimes, it seems very quiet. Lately, it really seemed quiet; I was seeing no results from all the prayers. However, I was led to realize that God had actually been quietly working all along, bringing results for which I had not given Him credit. I still had hope, and I didn't realize that the hope I had was because of all those subtle things that God had done in each situation.

I've been praying specific things for my family—Bob, David and Andrea, Susie and Jarrod, Tom and Jessica, Carlisle, Kendall, and Caitlin. I've been praying for people I met at my book signings. As a member of a store's author program, which was a huge blessing from God, I'm scheduled quite often at their grocery stores throughout the area. People coming to my table to hear about my book often share what's going on in their lives, and I do pray for them. On my list is for Genie's knee to be restored by God, comfort for a widower I met at another book signing, for contracts to go through for Paul. That prayer for Paul has been answered in a better way than we had imagined. These are just a few God-given connections from book signings. Oh, and don't forget to pray for yourself. Praise to God that my prayer that God would restore my left knee has been answered. That was one huge prayer answered.

God can go out of His way to connect people for His purpose. He did that by reconnecting Donna and me. It makes me smile to just think about it.

When I go into their store for a book signing, I ask the manager where to set up. One time, it was by a table full of Easter candy. Oh, boy. I sat there for two days, tempted by that chocolate. Then, suddenly, I heard someone at that Easter candy table talking to me.

Carlisle laughed as she said, "You probably thought the candy was talking to you, Grammy! 'Come, eat me!'"

It was Donna, not the Easter candy talking, telling me she recognized me from when I was at this same store almost a year before, signing my books. She told me how much she and her husband enjoyed my book, and that the meaning of *Restore* had become the focus of their prayers. We must have talked for two hours. The manager kept walking by, probably wondering what was going on, but he never said a word to us.

Donna and I have connected for lunch since and have enjoyed more talks. I've met her amazing teenage son. Donna and I both realize God connected us for a real purpose. I feel that way about everyone I have met—and especially those I have met through my books. Those books were inspired by God. I just got the privilege of writing them down. If they draw a reader and me together, I feel it is because of God.

As I sat reflecting on the joy of the Lord, I realized that I was so at peace. I said to the Lord, "Do You realize I haven't given up on seeing You move to restore all the needs of the people for whom I've been praying? I know You know me well enough that You're aware I can keep on praying for them for years. You, God, are the one Who pointed out so long ago that I believe in prayer and persevere in prayer."

Experience Him for yourself. God needs us to really get serious about which side of the fence we are on. Do you see what is going on in the world? God is indeed making a huge move to bring people to Himself. If you are following any of the prophetically gifted men and women of God, you are hearing the same thing from all of them. That's the Holy Spirit talking through all who will allow Him to do so. I love hearing others saying recently that limbs will be growing back, hospitals will be emptying, tsunami-type power of God is moving in. Exactly the same words, the same things God had me write in *Restore, Restore, Restore and More* in 2016. Oh, how I love confirmation. I knew it had to be from God, and these prophetic men and women speaking in 2018—the same exact thing I had already written—are confirming that indeed I have clearly heard from God. Both of my first two books were inspired by God, and this one is, as well. I have just written as quickly as the thoughts would come, and then I approached Carlisle so she could give a young view of it all. We did have some really quiet times, weeks with not knowing what to write, but with prayer came a release each time.

Around this same time, the Holy Spirit spoke to me through a sermon at church. The pastor was saying, "God totally loves it when we ask Him questions. He loves to answer our questions, so be alert for your answer." I love confirmation about what I'm learning from God, and that was more confirmation. No wonder the Holy Spirit made a big deal about it when I asked my question and when Carlisle asked hers. We both had forgotten about ours, but the Holy Spirit hadn't. Both of our questions were suddenly answered. He is happy when any of us come to Him for answers, rather than going from wave to wave, trying to find out.

The root of all sin is lack of prayer. It is a sign of self-sufficiency, of an I-don't-need-God attitude.

Prayer is indeed important, and interceding for others is, as well. Start the day with prayer, end the day with it, and write down the ways you have heard from God during the day. Enjoy the relationship, and don't make it a chore you have to check off your list. God sees right through that.

He will tell you that you are neither hot nor cold. This lukewarm state is nauseating to Him, and he wants to just spit you out of His mouth. Sound familiar? It's in the Bible.

"I know your deeds, that you are neither cold nor hot. I wish you were either one or the other! So, because you are lukewarm—neither hot nor cold—I am about to spit you out of my mouth" (Revelation 3:15–16 NIV).

I so believe God is serious about that, don't you? I believe that He is raising up a prayer army of children who pray with trust, belief, and confidence that God hears them, and He can do anything. Encourage your children to join that army of prayer warriors.

"Let the little children come to Me. Do not stop them. The holy nation of God is made up of ones like these" (Mark 10:14 NLV).

Enjoy your time in prayer.

Chapter 11

The Mustard Seed: Why Is Such a Tiny Seed Spoken of in the Bible?

God's Word tells us we just need a tiny bit of faith, the size of a mustard seed. That much faith can move a mountain.

I've seen a mustard seed. It is so very tiny. When I was ten and growing up in Oklahoma City, my mother gave me a mustard seed charm to add to my charm bracelet. That was over sixty years ago, and I still have that bracelet with that cherished charm on it. She explained that a tiny bit of faith, as small as a mustard seed, could move a mountain. Jesus makes that clear. We see that when we read the parable of the mustard seed. There is the comparison of that tiny seed bringing about great results. In the parable, Jesus said that tiny seed grew, resulting in a large tree where birds can nest.

After my mother explained the meaning, I told her that I had that much faith. I could move mountains. I was ten, sitting on her bed looking at the charm, and I knew then that my faith could move mountains. I remember thinking that if God said so, it was a fact.

I have since learned that it has to be God's power that moves the mountain, not mine. I must take my eyes off the mountain and keep them on Him.

That small beginning of faith—this tiny seed of faith—is given to each of us.

The Parable of the Mustard Seed

"He told them another parable: 'The kingdom of heaven is like a mustard seed, which a man took and planted in his field. Though it is the smallest of all seeds, yet when it grows, it is the largest of garden plants and becomes a tree, so that the birds come and perch in its branches'" (Matthew 13:31–32 NIV).

God has repeatedly told me through sermons, through scripture, through the Holy Spirit, to not despise small beginnings. A mustard seed is a small beginning, but that tiny bit of faith, when it is given to a child, can move mountains. They run with it, having no problem believing with excitement about God and His power. They believe God is amazing, real, and loving. A child hungers to know more.

Look at the little boy when Jesus asked for food (John 6:5–13). The boy had food. His mother had packed him five loaves and three fish to take with him. He had the solution and gave Jesus all he had. The child wasn't worried about being laughed at for this gift. That small amount of food was not a solution to an adult mind, but to that little boy, it was perfect for Jesus.

Let's read about it:

"When Jesus looked up and saw a great crowd coming toward him, he said to Philip, 'Where shall we buy bread for these people to eat?' He asked this only to test him, for he already had in mind what he was going to do.

"Philip answered him, 'It would take more than half a year's wages to buy enough bread for each one to have a bite!'

"Another of his disciples, Andrew, Simon Peter's brother, spoke up, 'Here is a boy with five small barley loaves and two small fish, but how far will they go among so many?'

"Jesus said, 'Have the people sit down.' There was plenty of grass in that place, and they sat down (about five thousand men were there). Jesus then took the loaves, gave thanks, and distributed to those who were seated as much as they wanted. He did the same with the fish.

"When they had all had enough to eat, he said to his disciples, 'Gather the pieces that are left over. Let nothing be wasted.' So they gathered them and filled twelve baskets with the pieces of the five barley loaves left over by those who had eaten" (John 6:5–13 NIV).

Indeed, it was perfect for Jesus. He fed five thousand (plus women and children) and had twelve baskets of food left over. Never despise small beginnings.

Matthew 18:3 tells us that Jesus loved for children to come to Him.

The disciples said, "Get away; Jesus is busy and has no time for you." Read what Jesus said when hearing them say that:

The Little Children and Jesus

"People were bringing little children to Jesus for him to place his hands on them, but the disciples rebuked them. When Jesus saw this, he was indignant. He said to them, 'Let the little children come to me, and do not hinder them, for the kingdom of God belongs to such as these'" (Mark 10:13–14 NIV).

Jesus said to let the children come to Him. Be like them. Read what Jesus said when asked who is the greatest in the kingdom of heaven:

The Greatest in the Kingdom of Heaven

"At that time the disciples came to Jesus and asked, 'Who, then, is the greatest in the kingdom of heaven?'

"He called a little child to him, and placed the child among them. And he said: 'Truly I tell you, unless you change and become like little children, you will never enter the kingdom of heaven. Therefore, whoever takes the lowly position of this child is the greatest in the kingdom of heaven. And whoever welcomes one such child in my name welcomes me'" (Matthew 18:1–5 NIV).

Small beginnings. What do children have?
They trust.
They live without complications.
They operate in humility.
They are content in the little things.
They have faith that moves mountains.
They believe that if God's Word says so, it is a fact.
They are not self-conscious about using their faith.

As I mentioned before, I'm a member of a store's author program, and when at a book signing, I have a wonderful chance to watch children who are grocery shopping with a parent. The parent is usually busy with the list, getting what is needed, but the children are in full action. I mean, full action. Children don't just walk. No, they dance, jump, to try to hit a store banner, skip, stop to look at eye-level displays full of toys or candy. Full motion and delight. They don't seem to have a care in the world, and they always smile at me. I love that. Some will come back to my table and talk to me, forcing their mom or dad to stop.

There are people who pass me with their noses in the air, set on not looking at me. One lady doing that actually ran her grocery cart right into another shopper. Just a point of information: If you see a setup in a store, we are asked to be there. Our books or products are in the store's database, and we are there to tell about them. Purchases from us are checked out. The shopper pays for my book through the store.

The same goes for the workers cutting the samples in stores for you to taste. They like to be smiled at, as well. It wouldn't hurt you to smile. I really don't know about those who give samples, whether they are employees of the store or independent representatives, but they are real people with feelings. They have been on their feet all day, and we have no idea if they are worried about a sick child or unpaid bills. Treat them with the same respect that you would like to receive.

Workers can tell when someone is on the phone or when shoppers are busy and just want to get out of there. I for sure can, and a smile from me most always gives me one in return as they hurry by. There are plenty of others who do have time to stop at my table to hear about my books. If they buy one, I offer to sign it. They often tell me about themselves, and I do remember their needs and pray for them.

As I said, children are delightful. They smile, wave, and keep looking back at me with that smile. No wonder Jesus loves them to come to Him. Children are so very kind. Watch children. See how quickly a smile forms on their lips. Let's be like them.

 A mustard seed is tiny. As long as you have the faith the size of a mustard seed, God can do amazing things through you. God can take that small faith and make it giant. As long as you have a tiny crack in your wall of doubt and shame, God can knock those doubts down.

In fifth grade, my faith grew from a mustard seed into a mountain. It has continued to grow. An example is that I used to read the Bible, but I didn't take a thing away from it. I used to skim over without a care. So I began to read just ten verses a day, and I found life-changing lessons each and every time. Now the Bible is new, real, and gives me life every time I open it (except when it comes to a list of names).

My prayers to Him have changed immensely. Before, I used to try to get through all the problems in my life so I could get to bed. Now I spend hours just talking to God and thanking Him. It's incredible. But this didn't happen until I read, making it a habit to read at least ten verses in the Bible, looking for God to give me life-changing lessons.

Carlisle learned to focus on God talking to her through the Bible, and since the Word is alive, God was able to let her realize He was indeed talking to her. Her prayer time became an intimate walk with God time. I hope this is a habit she keeps. That's what God wants from all of us. He wants us to realize He is talking to us in His Word, and He wants our prayer time to be special. He knows when you are indeed glad to talk to him, or if you are simply getting something checked off on your list of things to do. We don't want friends who feel they have to reach out to us so they can say, "That's done," and walk away. I don't want friends like that. I'm sure you don't. God doesn't, either.

God wants to grow our faith. It started out so tiny, but it isn't meant to stay that way. A tiny beginning is all that God needs to lead us to His purpose. Probably a dozen times this past year, God has reminded me to not despise these small beginnings.

I'm catching on now. There is a reason God starts us out with the small things. He watches our faith grow, and more and more is added. Mountains move now. Anything blocking the path God wants us to walk on is knocked down.

It is a battle, one that requires putting on our armor, reading the Word, and spending time in prayer. I'm talking about this faith walk. We can't do it alone. It is our faith in God that has grown and grown. Actually, it grows as fast as we allow it. We are the ones slowing us down. We are the ones who look to the world and get involved in the things of the world that the devil has purposely put there. Yes, we are in a battle with the ruler of the world, who is Satan.

Senseless time spent playing video games is exactly what Satan wants to see. As far as the enemy is concerned, the more time wasted in our day, the better.

The verse "Train up a child the way he should go, and when he is old he'll not depart from it" (Proverbs 22:6) comes to mind. God taught Carlisle, through her teacher, the joy of going deeper into His Word. Carli then realized that true prayer with God is a sincere talking and listening time. It's not just rambling off the needs of people, although that time of intercession is important too. True intercession time comes with a burden to pray for a certain person, and it is accompanied by an urgency to have God work in their situation. That's that intercession gift. More about that in the next chapters.

Nothing stops a child's faith from seeing results. My family often said that whatever I hoped to see would just work out. They didn't know, and I didn't know, that what was at full throttle was my childhood faith.

I prayed to God without putting any limits on Him. That's what Carlisle does all the time. With that kind of faith, God is able to do anything.

Go back to the small, pure beginning. Grab that mustard seed faith, and as a child does, run with it. Run without thinking of your job, stocks, family, health, or any other limitations your adult mind might consider. God tells us He knows our needs, has a wonderful plan, and simply wants us to trust Him.

Chapter 12

Teaching Your Child the Habit of Daily Prayer, from Discipline to Delight

I can't think of a better time to find the delight of a relationship with our heavenly Father than when we are young. There is delight in being with the Lord, talking to Him in prayer.

Psalm 37:4–6 talks about delight in the Lord:

"Take delight in the LORD, and he will give you the desires of your heart. Commit your way to the LORD; trust in him and he will do this: He will make your righteous reward shine like the dawn, your vindication like the noonday sun" (Psalm 37:4–6 NIV).

The last thing Satan wants us to do is pray, much less does he want us to make it a habit. Therefore, he makes it as hard as he can to concentrate, staying focused on the Lord in prayer.

Foundation of Prayers

The foundation of prayer is explained in Hebrews 11:6. God wants His children to come to Him:

"And without faith it is impossible to please God, because anyone who comes to him must believe that he exists and that he rewards those who earnestly seek him" (Hebrews 11:6 NIV).

Praying, coming to God in prayer, is earnestly seeking God, whom you love, whom you can't see, but whom by faith you know that He for sure is right there. This definitely pleases God. Does He hear us? Jesus told us that He does:

"I knew that you always hear me, but I said this for the benefit of the people standing here, that they may believe that you sent me" (John 11:42 NIV).

Where Do We Pray?

Jesus had a habit of going up on a hill early in the morning to be in prayer with His Father. He didn't take anyone, but went alone to enjoy His time with God.

Jesus Prays in a Solitary Place

"Very early in the morning, while it was still dark, Jesus got up, left the house and went off to a solitary place, where he prayed" (Mark 1:35 NIV).

"But Jesus often withdrew to lonely places and prayed" (Luke 5:16 NIV).

The first thing Jesus showed us by His example is to get off by ourselves. Where can children safely go to be alone in prayer with the Lord? They certainly can't wander off outside in the dark to pray, as Jesus did.

The Bible has the answer for this:

"But when you pray, go into your room, close the door and pray to your Father, who is unseen. Then your Father, who sees what is done in secret, will reward you" (Matthew 6:6 NIV).

We all can safely go into our room, close the door, and pray. Some have a prayer chair. Billy Graham suggests even a corner of a room. The King James Version (KJV) is even more specific about a room:

"But thou, when thou prayest, enter into thy closet, and when thou hast shut thy door, pray to thy Father which is in secret; and thy Father which seeth in secret shall reward thee openly" (Matthew 6:6).

Even today, many people have prayer closets. So let's talk about going into our closet, shutting the door, and praying. The point is that you have no one to distract you in this time with the Lord.

So here we are in our prayer closet. You may start off fine, praying to the Father, but then Satan starts to work to pull your focus away from that. He doesn't want you to focus on God in prayer, God seeing you pray, and God rewarding you. Why? Why does that bother Satan? It is because you will want to do it often, go to God alone in prayer. Soon, a habit of prayer will be established as you delight in your God time. Satan doesn't want that.

At a women's conference at our church about eight years ago, they started with the focus on praying by putting on this skit about prayer time alone with God. On stage, the actor had a desk and chair, and she was seated there with her Bible, a notebook, and a pen. This was clearly her set time and place to be with the Lord, and she arrived ready.

Sherri Kay, a name I just made up, starts out, "Dear heavenly Father, Thank you for this wonderful day. Please forgive me for any sins I have committed, for I don't want to be separated at all from you. I have so much to pray for. First, I want to pray for my family. I pray for ... oh, my family ... I need to take the meat out of the freezer so it will be thawed by tonight. I'll be right back, God.... Okay, I'm back. That didn't take long, and my family will have a good dinner now. I was praying for my family. I pray for my little Allison. Oh my! Allison has a birthday party after school, and I need to wrap that present. I will be right back, God!... Okay, I'm back. Allison will be proud to take that present I just wrapped to the party, God. I wrapped it like a professional department store gift wrapper. I can just see her taking it in. Back to praying, God. Let's see ...

where was I? Oh, I know. I pray for … oh, no! The dress Allison needs to wear to the party is in the washing machine. I need to go put those clothes in the dryer. I'll be back, Lord. Here I am, I am back, and we have so much to talk about. But, God, look at the time! I have to leave now for my hair appointment. I don't want to make my hairdresser run late for the rest of the day just because I was late. Then I would be late picking up the children at school, and Allison would be late taking that beautifully wrapped gift to the birthday party. I don't have time to talk to you right now, God. I'm sorry, but I must brush my hair and get out of this house."

There was a little laughter in the room, but uncomfortable laughter, for this was so familiar to all of us. You closed that closet door with full intention of turning to God in prayer, but the minutes passed, and there was not much of a thought of God, it seemed.

Could you visualize God in that little scene above? God was delighted Sherri Kay was there to be with Him, but there she goes. What are we putting before our time with God, having called Him to listen to our prayers, yet running out of the room to take care of this or that? What is God watching us do while He waits for this precious time with His child … with you, with me? What did we decide was much more important than talking to the Creator of the universe, our Creator? Oh, my. Yes, it has happened to me; what happened to Sherri Kay has happened to me too.

I have found that taking a prayer journal in hand and writing out my prayers keeps me focused. It is also a valuable record of what I prayed on which day, and as the answers come, I can record the answers. A true faith builder, that is. I also learned the secret of having a little notepad, so when a thought comes, like to put meat out to thaw or wrap a present, whatever needs to be taken care of, I simply write it down on the small notepad. It will wait, and I can take care of it after my time with God.

Providing preschool children with crayons and pads of paper allows them to draw a picture about what they are praying to God that day. It can be the child's record. Start them out with a short time, and allow them to lead you how to increase it. God does His part. He meets anyone who is seeking Him:

"Come near to God and he will come near to you" (James 4:8a NIV).

We know that Satan tries to stop us from prayer. Carlisle recently shared that even she has developed the wonderful time with God routine. Let's see what happened:

 Kendall and I are on a competitive cheer team, and we practice for several hours, five days a week. My right arm started to hurt, but it wasn't swollen. We didn't think it was a problem, but it got worse. My mom took me to the sports medicine doctor, and he told us I had injured my growth plate. I had to wear a cast for two weeks, and that meant I couldn't cheer. I went to practice and walked through the motions, but I felt lonely and left out. Two weeks later, the cast was off, but a splint was put on with orders for no cheering yet. We had our first competition coming up that Kendall and I could be a part of since joining the team. She cheered with the team in that competition, but I had to walk to the back of the stage and kneel when the tumbling and lifting parts were going on. That was the end of November 2017. During all these weeks, I still prayed, but I had lost my close relationship, that connection with God. I was feeling out of place, broken, and alone. When things are going good, life is great, being happy with God, and the time with Him is easy. During the month when doing what I loved to do taken away from me, I forgot God was there for me. I was just going through the motions of prayer and Bible reading. I picked up a devotional and read John 10:14. It says, "I am the Good Shephard. My sheep know my voice and I know them." I memorized this verse and I remembered God had a plan. I remembered He was with me, and I remembered He loved me. These three simple facts you probably hear all the time. God has a plan for you, He is with you, and He loves you. But, when you feel all alone, out of place, and broken you take your eyes off God I guess. That's when you

most need to tap into the love God has for you. Instead of turning to look at what you are being left out of, turn to those three facts I spoke about. You'll see the true power of those small words. This is my life experience that will help me. I have to tell you that I did get to tumble and cheer in the next competition we had in December of 2017. I have a splint I wear at all times for now, and I have to ice my arm before tumbling, but I don't have to kneel at the back during part of our routine. I was in ALL of it, and I got to stand with the team to have our picture taken as All Star Level 1 Grand Champion Team 2017.

God got Carlisle back to the positive (He is so good at that), so let's turn to the positive. What does God do when we pray? He delights when we come to Him, so how does God encourage us to make that a habit? This is happy thinking, for God so loves it when we come to Him in prayer. There is joy in the Lord. It's fun to hang around someone full of joy, and God makes it a delight to hang around Him. God delights in us so much that He sings a song over you. I have indeed experienced that and told that story in my other books. These verses will convince you our God is blessed and happy:

"Do not grieve, for the joy of the LORD is your strength" (Nehemiah 8:10 NIV).

"The LORD your God is with you, the Mighty Warrior who saves. He will take great delight in you; in his love he will no longer rebuke you, but will rejoice over you with singing" (Zephaniah 3:17 NIV).

"I have told you this so that my joy may be in you and that your joy may be complete" (John 15:11 NIV).

How Long Should a Child Pray?

Have your child start out praying to God for five minutes. That time can increase as the child leads you. It will be God pressing into them, meeting them where they are, doing the work now. He'll be the one developing this wonderful time of talking to the Creator of the universe. This habit, started while they are young, can lead to a God-directed life and reaching one's full potential.

Show them a verse on prayer that they can focus on, a promise in a prayer that they can claim. Let the Bible be very much a part of their prayer time. Even young children can memorize Bible verses. I've heard a group of five-year-olds recite from memory long chapters from the Bible, right along with older schoolchildren. They probably learn it easier than the older children.

Even young children recognize when God has answered a prayer, and they delight in that. My friend's two-year-old grandson prayed with his grandmother for his dad to quit having back pain. They prayed that his dad would be well by the time he got back home. When the child was back home, he asked his dad how he felt. His dad started to complain, but his eyes got wide, and he said, "I actually feel fine. I'm not hurting at all."

My friend said that this little boy bent his arm, made a fist, and said, "Yes. God did it."

Do you suppose that little child will want to pray again? Yes, indeed. He now knows the power of prayer. You can't start too young to teach them.

Perhaps this is an ah-ha moment for you. You wondered why you started out with the best intentions to pray, yet realized an hour later that perhaps you only prayed a sentence or two. What happened to that precious time you wanted with the Lord? Was your armor on? Were you delighting in the Lord or just feeling an obligation to check prayer time off? God sees right through your motives.

"When you ask, you do not receive, because you ask with wrong motives, that you may spend what you get on your pleasures" (James 4:3 NIV).

If that has ever happened to you, then you can make this a teaching time for you as well as your child, developing a habit of delight in time with God. That is what He wants, and that is what you want. Prayer is a marvelous time, yet a mystery. Why would God want to talk to us? That's part of the mystery, but the Bible says He does. He hears our prayers and answers them.

"The eyes of the LORD are on the righteous, and his ears are attentive to their cry" (Psalm 34:15 NIV).

"Go back and tell Hezekiah, the ruler of my people, 'This is what the LORD, the God of your father David, says: I have heard your prayer and seen your tears; I will heal you.' On the third day from now you will go up to the temple of the LORD" (2 Kings 20:5 NIV).

"But God has surely listened and has heard my prayer" (Psalm 66:19 NIV).

"They were helped in fighting them, and God delivered the Hagrites and all their allies into their hands, because they cried out to him during the battle. He answered their prayers, because they trusted in him" (1 Chronicles 5:20 NIV).

When you are focused in prayer, pressing into God, I know from experience that God can make that a time of delight. It can be a time of singing with God, a song that comes into your mind that you had forgotten about but love. Sing that song to God. God is exceptional at making things rhyme. I thought I was imagining that until I heard so many others repeat what God had told them, and it rhymed. That's God having fun with us.

It can be a time of revelation; perhaps God will lead you in a game that you delight in and play with Him, letting you know how to pray for someone. This has happened with me. God knows you so well, that He knows how to delight you, how to reach you so you can glorify Him.

As prayers are answered, you write them in your journal. Trust me, you think you can remember, but in time, you'll wish you had written the details down, for they fade over the year. Indeed, a prayer journal is valuable.

God time is such a happy time; the closer you get to Him, it becomes sheer delight. He can make you laugh by reminding you of delightful times. You then are forming a habit of prayer, of the God time when you can't wait to go to your heavenly Father in prayer. You may find yourself praying two or three hours in your time with the Lord. I have, as have many. Martin Luther King is widely quoted as having said, "I have so much to do that I shall have to spend the first three hours in prayer." You'll find, too, the value of quiet time alone with God. Yes, teach your children this wonderful habit early.

Chapter 13

Fruit of the Spirit versus Gifts of the Holy Spirit

Two Baskets

Two baskets full of gifts?

No, but two pretend baskets to help us realize the difference between fruit and gifts. The Holy Spirit is known for producing the fruit of the Spirit in us and also for giving us gifts according to however He wants to give us those gifts. That's why I said to pretend there are two baskets the Holy Spirit carries. It's easy to separate the two groups if we put them in imaginary baskets.

Fruit of the Spirit in Us

Fruit of the Spirit in us? Apples, grapes, oranges, pears kind of fruit?

No, but the fruit of the Spirit is what it is called. Fruit really is a characteristic of Jesus. The Holy Spirit produces in us the characteristics that Jesus has, if we allow ourselves to be filled each day with the Holy Spirit.

What are the characteristics of Jesus? I always remember them by saying this sentence:

"Lord Jesus, please let God get from me thanks." I'll explain.

Lord, the L stands for **Love.**

Jesus, the J stands for **Joy.**

Please, the P stands for **Peace.**

Let, the L stands for **Longsuffering** (or patience).

God, the G stands for **Goodness.**

Get, this G stands for **Gentleness.**

From, the F stands for **Faithfulness.**

Me, the M stands for **Meekness** (or subdued, easygoing).

Thanks, the T stands for **Temperance** (or self-control).

Now, this little mnemonic only works with the King James Version of Galatians 5:22–23. If you use another translation of the Bible, you will have to make up your own memory help sentence.

I will show you. Here is the King James Version:

"But the fruit of the Spirit is love, joy, peace, longsuffering, gentleness, goodness, faith, Meekness, temperance: against such there is no law" (Galatians 5:22–23).

Here is a more modern translation, the New International Version:

"But the fruit of the Spirit is love, joy, peace, forbearance, kindness, goodness, faithfulness, gentleness and self-control. Against such things there is no law."

This one ends with "self-control." Self-control is used in our vocabulary more than the word *temperance.* They both mean the same thing. My little sentence won't work on the New International Version.

Jesus is so kind, and our goal is to be that way, too. When someone hurts us in anyway, our flesh just wants to be mad at them and put them down with our words, but the Holy Spirit teaches us that Jesus says to pray for our enemies. Do good to those who hate you. This is found in Luke:

Love for Enemies

"But to you who are listening I say: Love your enemies, do good to those who hate you, bless those who curse you, pray for those who mistreat you. If someone slaps you on one cheek, turn to them the other also. If someone takes your coat, do not withhold your shirt from them. Give to everyone who asks you, and if anyone takes what belongs to you, do not demand it back. Do to others as you would have them do to you.

"If you love those who love you, what credit is that to you? Even sinners love those who love them. And if you do good to those who are good to you, what credit is that to you? Even sinners do that. And if you lend to those from whom you expect repayment, what credit is that to you? Even sinners lend to sinners, expecting to be repaid in full. But love your enemies, do good to them, and lend to them without expecting to get anything back. Then your reward will be great, and you will be children of the Most High, because he is kind to the ungrateful and wicked. Be merciful, just as your Father is merciful" (Luke 6:27–36 NIV).

This reminds me of a verse that tells us to turn the other cheek. That's in Matthew 5:39. This is something that has always confused me.

"But I tell you, do not resist an evil person. If anyone slaps you on the right cheek, turn to them the other cheek also."(NIV)

It says to turn the other cheek also, so does that mean you are not supposed to protect yourself if someone is going to hurt you? The answer is no. This is metaphorical, which I literally just figured out, showing us to not slap them back but forgive them. For example, my little sister came into a room at school, and three of her friends were talking about her, and they were saying mean things about her, not knowing she was there hearing them. Kendall was hurt and angry, and wanted to say mean things right back. But this verse is telling her that's not the way to react. She is to turn the other cheek, in other words, to forgive. See, it is easy to pray for them because that is an action you can force yourself to do. You can't force yourself to love someone. I can pray for my enemy, but I can't force myself to love my enemy. That would be hard for Kendall to do as well.

Carlisle just now figured out, on her own, that she wasn't to take that verse literally. It is a point of confusion. I believe that Jesus's teaching in this passage is to let go of the desire to get back at the ones hurting you. That is what the flesh wants to do, but the influence of the Holy Spirit gives Christians the power to forgive, to "turn the other cheek," as Jesus says. It's mainly concerned with the issue of not retaliating or getting personal revenge.

In the case of self-defense, children should not be expected to stand quietly while someone attacks them physically. They should be trained to respond quickly to save themselves from danger. A loud scream, running to a safe adult, or other options that are appropriate should be taught to children by parents or by police visiting the school to talk to them about this. I'm so glad Carli brought this up, for it is such a good point, and one I had not thought about until now.

See, it is easy to pray for them because that is an action you can force yourself to do. You can't force yourself to love someone. I can pray for my enemy, but I can't force myself to love my enemy. That would be hard for Kendall to do as well.

That's why God gave us the supernatural power of the Holy Spirit inside of us to enable us to love them through Him. Yes, it seems a bit of a mystery, but when we are in tune to the Holy Spirit and under the influence of His leading, we can do all sorts of things not possible for us in our own flesh. God thought of everything we would need, and He has provided us with the very Spirit of His Son in us to be able to accomplish these. That is why we so need to awaken to God's Spirit of resurrection power that raised Jesus to life, now inside of us, and let Him empower our lives.

"So then beloved ones, the flesh has no claims on us at all, and we have no further obligation to live in obedience to it. For when you live controlled by the flesh, you are about to die. But if the Spirit puts to death the corrupt ways of the flesh, we then taste His abundant life" (Romans 8:12–13 The Passion Translation).

Living an abundant life sounds like what we all want to do. The Word of God tells us how that is possible. Yield yourself to the Holy Spirit, whom God puts inside every one of us who accept Christ as their personal Savior.

I put the whole context in Luke 6:27–36 above so that you can read why Jesus says to do that. By acting like Jesus would, we are rewarded by God. God gives the best kind of rewards, and God is whom we want to please.

Are you curious as to why Jesus's characteristics are referred to as fruit? The Bible explains that, as well. Let's read it in The Message translation:

The Vine and the Branches

"I am the Real Vine and my Father is the Farmer. He cuts off every branch of me that doesn't bear grapes. And every branch that is grape-bearing he prunes back so it will bear even more. You are already pruned back by the message I have spoken.

"Live in me. Make your home in me just as I do in you. In the same way that a branch can't bear grapes by itself but only by being joined to the vine, you can't bear fruit unless you are joined with me.

"I am the Vine, you are the branches. When you're joined with me and I with you, the relation intimate and organic, the harvest is sure to be abundant. Separated, you can't produce a thing. Anyone who separates from me is deadwood, gathered up and thrown on the bonfire. But if you make yourselves at home with me and my words are at home in you, you can be sure that whatever you ask will be listened to and acted upon. This is how my Father shows who he is—when you produce grapes, when you mature as my disciples.

"I've loved you the way my Father has loved me. Make yourselves at home in my love. If you keep my commands, you'll remain intimately at home in my love. That's what I've done—kept my Father's commands and made myself at home in his love.

"I've told you these things for a purpose: that my joy might be your joy, and your joy wholly mature. This is my command: Love one another the way I loved you. This is the very best way to love. Put your life on the line for your friends. You are my friends when you do the things I command you. I'm no longer calling you servants because servants don't understand what their master is thinking and planning. No, I've named you friends because I've let you in on everything I've heard from the Father.

"You didn't choose me, remember; I chose you, and put you in the world to bear fruit, fruit that won't spoil. As fruit bearers, whatever you ask the Father in relation to me, he gives you.

"But remember the root command: Love one another" (John 15:1–17).

I can't explain it any better than God did. Since fruit grows on a tree, God compares Himself to a tree, and we are the branches. This makes sense now. Since we become part of His tree when we accept Jesus as our personal Savior, we should bear the kind of fruit God would. Jesus shows us that. If we are not bearing fruit, as any gardener would do, we are cut back or, worse, cut off.

 In the verses 1 through 8, God is compared to a vine, and we are branches all coming off the vine. If we stay with God and listen to God, we are a branch that is able to bear fruit. A branch cannot bear fruit without a vine. We cannot bear the fruits, like the fruit of joy, or find true happiness and blessings for ourselves and others. It says if we stay true to God, we will get these blessings and bear fruit. The verses also tell us that we must love one another as God has loved us. Also, without God as our vine, we as branches will fall off or be cut off because we bear no fruit, and then

we are burned up by the world. Without God, we are left to a world that doesn't care about us, but God does love us.

Carlisle and I so don't want to be cut off from God, and I know you don't, either. So the best thing to do is learn about the work of the Holy Spirit. We are told be filled overflowing with the supernatural power of the Holy Spirit. Under the Holy Spirit's influence, we begin to bear fruit like Jesus did and glorify God.

 Verses 9 and 10 talk about God's love. God's love never, ever changes. It can't grow because it is at the highest possible level and beyond that. It can't lessen, because He loves us unconditionally. Just think about that, because Jesus's and God's love for us is the only thing that will never change.

If we could only grasp how much God loves us, if only our faith would allow us to accept just how much God loves us, we would be able to pass His love so very easily to others. God doesn't love us based on what we can do for Him. He loves us because God is love. We don't have to perform a certain way; we don't have to earn the love of God. We just have to let ourselves experience the fullness of that love God has for us. Paul prayed that for the Ephesians, so Paul must have been able to receive the fullness of God's love. Read with me Ephesians 3:14–19:

A Prayer for the Ephesians

"For this reason I kneel before the Father, from whom every family in heaven and on earth derives its name. I pray that out of his glorious riches he may strengthen you with power through his Spirit in your inner being, so that Christ may dwell in your hearts through faith. And I pray that you, being rooted and established in love, may have power, together with all the Lord's holy people, to grasp how wide and long and high and deep is the love of Christ, and to know this love that surpasses knowledge—that you may be filled to the measure of all the fullness of God" (Ephesians 3:14–19 NIV).

All He asks of us is that we love one another.

The first part of verse 16 is super cool, like it should be the last scene of an extremely emotional action movie: "You didn't choose me, remember; I chose you." Also, if you think about it, it's incredible: the God of the universe, who breathes out stars that are around 1.83544 trillion times bigger than the Earth, chose you. You are a random human that is one billion times smaller than width of the sun, and the sun isn't even a particularly large star, yet 1,300,000 planet Earths can fit inside of it. He created the sun with three, no four words: "Let there be light." Seriously, the sun is one billion times wider than a human. God created this whole universe, and then He created us.

All He asks of us, after all that, is that we love one another.

That reminds me of something my teacher said that has stuck with me. She said that we don't have the right to hold a grudge. We don't have the right not to forgive someone.

The Gifts of the Spirit

Concerning Spiritual Gifts

"Now about the gifts of the Spirit, brothers and sisters, I do not want you to be uninformed. You know that when you were pagans, somehow or other you were influenced and led astray to mute idols. Therefore I want you to know that no one who is speaking by the Spirit of God says, 'Jesus be cursed,' and no one can say, 'Jesus is Lord,' except by the Holy Spirit.

"There are different kinds of gifts, but the same Spirit distributes them. There are different kinds of service, but the same Lord. There are different kinds of working, but in all of them and in everyone it is the same God at work.

"Now to each one the manifestation of the Spirit is given for the common good. To one there is given through the Spirit a message of wisdom, to another a message of knowledge by means of the same Spirit, to another faith by the same Spirit, to another gifts of healing by that one Spirit, to another miraculous powers, to another prophecy, to another distinguishing between spirits, to another speaking in different kinds of tongues, and to still another the interpretation of tongues. All these are the work of one and the same Spirit, and he distributes them to each one, just as he determines" (1 Corinthians 12:1–11 NIV).

If you counted them, you would see the Bible tells us in this chapter about nine gifts that the Holy Spirit passes out to the children of God. We will look at these, and then go to other books of the Bible that tells us about even more gifts. Let's learn about these nine for now:

"To one there is given through the Spirit a message of wisdom."

People with this gift are able to take the gospel and help others apply it to their everyday lives. This gift lets you visualize how something is to be done before it's even started, and you intuitively seem to know the most effective course of action from among several choices. Your gift of wisdom will enable you to so easily see a truth that you may find it incredible that others fail to see this, so you need to be sensitive to the Holy Spirit guiding you. You want to be compassionate as well as patient. People often come to you to help them, for this gift lets you apply biblical knowledge to their problem. The solution you suggest usually turns out well. This wonderful gift works in a very natural way. It is so natural that you may not even realize, until later, that you were acting supernaturally with your gifting. You think about it later and realize you didn't have all the facts, yet you knew exactly what to do. That was the gift of wisdom given to you by the Holy Spirit at work.

"To another a message of knowledge by means of the same Spirit."

Sometimes, the word of knowledge and the word of wisdom are dual gifts that work together. Wisdom is actually knowledge in action, so a word of wisdom tells someone what to do in the situation.

I was given a word of knowledge one day, and I had no idea what my directions meant, nor did I realize it was a word of knowledge being given to me. I heard to pray "the connection prayer." I had never heard of a connection prayer, nor did I know a way to pray it. The only thing I could think to say was, "I pray the connection prayer." That was it. I then went on about my day, and later our daughter called. She told me she was at a client's office to pick up a check, and a man came in to do what he needed and left. However, this man came back in and told her that he was in his car and heard the Holy Spirit ask him if he was going to follow directions or not. So the man came back in and delivered a message from God to Susie that she desperately needed to hear. I don't even remember what the message was, but it was hugely important to her to hear that day. The connection prayer got this man and our daughter in the same office at the same time so that this word from the Lord could be delivered. Amazing. That is a real example of the Spiritual gift of the word of knowledge. It was a subtle thought and very clear as to what I was to do (pray the connection prayer), even if I had no understanding of what on earth that was. I received information from the Spirit that I didn't acquire through natural means.

 That is getting it done to just say the words, even if you don't know what they mean.

"To another faith by the same Spirit."

Faith is my main gift, and I wouldn't know what to do without it. I thank God often for this precious gift of faith, which has always been such a part of me. My faith helps simplify life, because I can trust God to take care of everything. My family often spoke about things just always working out for me. I had no clue then that was my gift of faith working at full throttle, but I do know that now. The only thing now is that since I know God can and will take care of what I have asked, even in difficult times, why does He sometimes take so long? Have you been there, getting very impatient for the answer? I get reminded—by the scriptures, by the Holy Spirit, by other people—that God has perfect timing. Yes, but why can't it be now? I need patience as one of my gifts. Clearly, patience is not one of my gifts.

 Patience isn't my gift, either. I recently was in a situation that needed a lot of patience. I hurt my wrist at cheerleading practice, and at this time in my life, everything was falling into place. Then, everything fell apart in an instant, and I couldn't fix it. I knew God could, though, so I asked Him to heal me, to make everything better. He didn't heal me that day. Why didn't He? It made me feel sad, angry, forgotten, but then I remembered all I had to do was to trust and be patient. In the end, God answered my prayer, in time to cheer with the team when we won Grand Champions for Level One. It was one of the biggest prayers ever answered in my life. It was two days before the competition, and nobody, not the doctor, or my mom, or my dad, thought I could compete, and neither did I. I had asked God that even if He didn't heal me until after that, I would be able to compete. Then I was given a brace that enabled me to compete. I actually didn't figure out this prayer had been answered until a couple of weeks later. I thanked God, and I've learned so much. God has His perfect timing, and He likes to teach us patience along the way. So just remember that in the end, God's timing is always perfect for everything, even if it seems you have to wait forever. He always answers prayers.

I need to tell you that all the gifts of the Spirit move through a yielded and obedient person. How do you know if you are a yielded person? You will possess the fruit of the Spirit controlling you. When the gift of faith is at work, the believer has supernatural belief to trust God for everything (that is, if you keep your adult faith from complicating things). The pure, childlike faith lets the gift of faith move freely. If God said it, it will happen. If God wrote it down, you can stand firmly on that Word. With this gift of faith, you naturally know God has this situation in His hands, whatever the situation is. There is no need to doubt, so just delight in the relationship with the one you can so trust, your heavenly Father. Delight in the joy of that relationship. There is no need to fear. On the contrary, you never want to fear anything you have handed over to God. Why? This fear cancels out faith, and the gift of faith can't work. Remember this verse in 2 Timothy:

"For God hath not given us the spirit of fear; but of power, and of love, and of a sound mind" (2 Timothy 1:7 KJV).

Enjoy your gift of faith if the Holy Spirit chose to give that to you. Use it to encourage the body of Christ. Help them to rest on your faith if theirs fails. This will happen as often as you allow, and you will find that your faith is strong enough to hold you both upright. When someone is leaning on your faith, you'll find yourself spending a lot more time enjoying reading the Bible. That's my experience, anyway. I guess this is a natural response, like knowing to drink more water when you are thirsty. This pull to read the Bible must be God's way of making sure you're refilling your mind so your faith does stay strong enough for the both of you.

"To another gifts of healing by that one Spirit."

This gift of healing is another of my gifts. People often have both the gift of faith and the gift of healing. They have an unwavering belief that God, through the Holy Spirit, will bring about healing to a person in need, sometimes by a supernatural means, other times through a doctor, the natural way. One rainy day, I slipped on the wet sidewalk, and I fell so fast it was startling. I knew immediately that my arm was broken, but my first thought was that God would take care of it. He did, through the talents of the orthopedic surgeon and the physical therapy staff. It was my right arm, and I'm right handed, so it stopped everything for a while. It delayed the writing of this book, and I had to cancel six book signings and a book festival for I couldn't use my right hand to sign. If I tried to with my left, it looked like a four-year-old had gotten ahold of my pen. (You should see my calendar during this time.) God did take care of me, and my arm is back to normal with full range of motion. I'm very thankful for that healing.

You may think, *Well, that is just normal; the gift of healing wasn't used.* Oh, yes it was. I spoke a few seconds after the fall that God would heal this arm. Just because it wasn't an instant supernatural happening doesn't mean God didn't work on my faith in this gift. The surgeon is very pleased with his work, for this was not a simple fracture, and the anticipated one-hour surgery took three. But the doctor was able to put me back together beautifully, and the proof is in the x-ray. You cannot even see the scars on the top and bottom of my wrist. The physical therapists were very pleased with how fast my range of motion came back. Don't discredit God's work. Give Him praise for each little improvement seen on each day.

 Also remember to thank God for the little things.

Remember to thank God for little things, like when you are feeling a little better, or when you are late to something. Yes, even thank God when you get delayed, because you might find that if you hadn't been delayed, you would have been in an accident. In the morning, the really early morning before everyone is up, I watch the world wake up. I thank God for all of it. I see how many details I can find, like the beautiful painted sky, and how the grass is greener on the rim of our fence, fading into yellow. Then there is almost a line where our civilized world touches God's nature.

You really do notice little details, Carlisle. Our God is amazing at details, but these little details are the things we sometimes miss, like the daily little improvements in our bodies. That verse comes to my mind again to never despise small beginnings.

There are supernatural healings, and they are amazing to see. Carlisle and I both would love to have that happen, when I broke my arm in August, and when Carlisle hurt her arm in November. We both would have liked to see a snap-of-the-finger type healing, but we thanked God for the timely healings we did get. Some healings are creative miracles, such as an eye growing back, limbs growing out, cancer falling off. I believe that we will be seeing more and more of these creative miracles because God wants heads turning back to Him. He wants a relationship with us, and He wants to bless us. Watch with me for these to happen, but celebrate the way our body can heal itself. I praise God that my body knew how to fix that painful broken arm once the doctor set it.

Celebrate the way our body can heal itself.

Yes, our body is incredible. It can put itself back together, and if you look closer, you can see God's signature on you. For example, laminin. Laminin is the stuff that is literally holding you together right now. Guess what? The laminin that is holding you together is in your body right now, and it is shaped like a cross. Laminin is like the glue that keeps the cells in place so that they work properly. It really is shaped like a cross. It's God's signature that He is actually holding us together. We saw a film about this in school.

Carlisle, I am so glad you had learned about that in school and thought to include this point. I just recently learned of this through a minister I follow, or I wouldn't know what you were talking about. It was on YouTube, and He had the picture of laminin (which you can google). You'll see that indeed it is shaped like a cross. He also had a picture of the laminin on an actual cell under a microscope, and there it was, the shape of the cross. God is so fun, and He is certainly the God of letting us know that the smallest detail is important to Him. He thought to put His signature on each and every cell of our body, holding it where it needs to be. I am so glad you are writing this book with me, Carli, for you think of things that I just had not thought of to include.

Stand on the healing scriptures in the Bible. Speak those over yourself rather than owning what Satan wants to have you think. Our words are powerful, and we get what we speak forth. Someone with the gift of healing can pray for you, but if you own what the enemy has thrown at you instead, you've taken over with your words. If the doctor says you have three months to live, and that is what you are telling everyone, you will be right. However, if you have been told that, but you are standing on the healing promises of God and speaking what God says out, the healing can take place. I was praying for two young adults at the same time who had been told their condition was terminal, and they had a short time left. One was constantly telling everyone that her time was short; the other was speaking forth those healing promises. Guess who is alive and well today? Yes, the one who spoke only what God said in His Word. (I will list those healing scriptures in the Endnotes at the back of the book.)

People with the gift of healing are very compassionate for those who are sick, and so knowing that without a doubt God can heal them, they delight in praying for that healing. Peter was like that. We read about Peter walking by a beggar and stopping. He knew the power of God was in him, and so Peter offered his hand, helped the beggar up, and said to walk. This man had been lame since birth, never had taken a step in his life, but was walking and jumping and praising God. Sometimes, just their touch is a healing touch, or a spoken word will result in the healing. (See Acts 3: 1-7)

This gift of healing is found in children as young as two. God's using their simple pure faith to show the world His power. It is a wonderful gift, but you have to be cautious that you are so firmly believing that you just presume God will move as you pray. God knows the big picture and has the entire circumstance in control. You, not having all the information, cannot be presumptuous about God.

The Holy Spirit helps you develop this gift so it can successfully be used for the body of Christ. I have been prone to do that, to be too optimistic of the power of God to move on my prayer, and had to be corrected. Thankfully, the Holy Spirit is a good teacher and gives gifts to those who will use them for encouraging and helping others. You will learn to be in tune to when the anointing of the Holy Spirit is there for you to use this gift, for then the Holy Spirit will be moving through you, and it will be manifested. Cherish this gift, and learn from the Holy Spirit how to use it successfully.

"To another prophecy."

This is a gift that I have only had for about sixteen years. I had not been very confident in this gift until I used it to write *Restore, Restore, Restore and More*. When it first came out, I was told my book was very prophetic. Now, a year later, I know that those who said it was prophetic were right. I am hearing the same words now, at the end of 2017, and it's been a year. I'm hearing Christian pastors and teachers say over and over the same words that God had me write in my book in 2016. They are being spoken out from people of God all over the world. I mean, they are really using the same words I heard as I wrote. They didn't all read my book, but we all have the same Holy Spirit. I am hearing them say God is coming fast, like the power of a tsunami wave; limbs are going to be growing out, hospitals emptying. You need to be alert so you don't miss this blessed move. I hear them say all these things that are chapters in my book, and I think to myself, *That is exactly what God had me write! That is what He led me to say. Restore, Restore, Restore and More* is a very prophetic book. I had no natural way to know what God's move was going to be. It was just very clear to me what I was hearing, and I wrote down what God was saying. The second day out, it made the Amazon bestseller list. I can't take credit for that. That has to be God at work.

We are going to see the supernatural power of God.

That is all so incredible, and I fully believe it all.

Prophecy is a gift that is unique and extraordinary. Paul speaks of it as one to be desired:

"Follow the way of love and eagerly desire gifts of the Spirit, especially prophecy" (Corinthians 14:1).

Revelations received by one with this gift edify or warn the church, but all prophecy must be tested to see that it does line up with the scriptures. We need to know that it was of God, not from just a human mind.

When I got called out by name and given my first prophecy in 1996, the prophet spoke about many things that would be occurring in my life, and nine of those things have already happened. For example, that man didn't know me at all, but one of the things he said was that God would be showing me why things had been the way they were before my next birthday, and indeed I was shown from some verses in Psalms why things had been as they were. I was shown those verses the night before my next birthday, in May 1996. Talk about coming down to the last minute; God does that a lot. Eight other things have already come true, as well. I am still waiting for the last, but I have not wavered, not doubted that I will see that too. It will be soon, because the timing appears to be now. (I thought God meant then, 1996. Nope, he meant all these years later, when it was the right time.)

It is very edifying to realize that God knows your name, does have a plan for your life and wants to see you walk in it. Don't despise that gift of prophecy. Paul said to desire it. It may be totally out of your comfort zone to walk in this gift but amazing for your own personal faith to know you really heard truth from the Lord. Known prophets of this day have thought they had heard but failed. They tell people they did fail, that what they thought was a clear revelation from the Lord was not. The Holy Spirit enabled them to learn what went wrong, and they moved on. Their gift had to be developed, as does ours. As the Holy Spirit develops this gift in you, you will be such an encouragement to the body of Christ.

Children are getting this prophetic gift, and we are not taking them seriously. Are you a parent of one of these children? Help them grow in their gift. Before they go to bed, ask them if there is any person they are thinking about, someone God put on their mind. They probably will tell you a name, but if not, that's fine. If a person was on their mind, ask if God is telling them anything about that person, and this will help them learn how to get used to hearing from God. God is speaking through the children of this generation. It's amazing. Pay attention to things they say. If it matches God's Words, has the authority that it will have being from the Holy Spirit in them, pay attention to them. God just may be talking to you, and I believe you will for sure know if it's indeed from God.

God loves children and wants us to help him.

This is one of my favorite things, that God loves children. As a child, one of the biggest things to us is just to be heard, for someone to just listen to us. God does.

Don't seek to live your life day by day by a prophetic message. God wants to listen to you and wants you to seek to hear Him for yourself through the Bible and a relationship with Him. Yes, every once in a while, He will send a prophetic message, but don't count on it every day. I, for one, have had only four prophetic messages given to me in all my years. It's my time with the Lord that guides me 99 percent of the time. If you have this gift and sense someone following you to just hear what you hear from God, teach them through the Bible and in their own personal quiet time with the Lord.

God knows my name.

God knows my name. It's all very incredible. I remember the night that I truly understood how awesome it is. That was after watching a Louie Giglio video at school. That was the video I saw where I learned about laminin holding us together and being the shape of the cross. His video just showed us how small we were, because seriously we are tiny, and how awesomely stupendous and amazing God is. I just understood how incredible it is that out of 7.4 billion people in the world (that's 7,400,000,000), God knows my name. He hears me when I speak to Him, and cares enough to help us write this book to get a message out about a tiny sliver of the incredible things He can do.

"To another distinguishing between spirits [gift of discernment]."

One with the gift of discernment is being able to see through deceit and phoniness even before it is evident to others. They can readily distinguish between spiritual truth and error, good and evil. They are usually able to correctly judge a person's character based on first impression, sensing if demonic forces are at work in them. They discern that a teaching is not true to the Bible. In other words, these people see beneath the surface of things, listening to both God and humans.

"To another speaking in different kinds of tongues."

"He who speaketh in an unknown tongue edifieth himself, but he who prophesieth edifies the church" (1 Corinthians 14:4 KJV).

When we pray in tongues (an unknown language), we edify ourselves. The Holy Spirit is praying, and the first time this happened was when Jesus told His disciples to wait in Jerusalem until they were filled with the power from on high. This is found in Luke 24:49–51:

"'And, Behold, I send the promise of my Father upon you: but tarry ye in the city of Jerusalem, until ye be endued with power from on high.' And he led them out as far as to Bethany, and he lifted up his hands, and blessed them. And it came to pass, while he blessed them, he was parted from them, and carried up into heaven."

So they waited there as they were commanded; let's see what happened.

"And when the day of Pentecost was fully come, they were all with one accord in one place, and suddenly there came a sound from heaven as a rushing mighty wind, and it filled all the house where they were sitting. And there appeared unto them cloven Tongues like as of fire, and it sat upon each of them. And they were all filled with the Holy Spirit, and began to speak with other Tongues, as the Spirit gave them utterance" (Acts 2:1–4 KJV).

How does this edify you, when you have no idea what you are saying? Very good question. Whatever took place by those speaking in tongues, the Holy Spirit speaking through all of them, they were different people. They were bold, speaking with authority from God, and the Bible said that three thousand people were saved.

When we speak with the gift of tongues, the Holy Spirit is speaking directly to God, but through us. The Holy Spirit and God are talking about something prepared for us that we have no idea about, and therefore, we cannot interfere with it by inserting our own limited understanding.

Our faith is built up as we pray in tongues. Jude 20–21 tells us that:

"But you, dear friends, by building yourselves up in your most holy faith and praying in the Holy Spirit, keep yourselves in God's love as you wait for the mercy of our Lord Jesus Christ to bring you to eternal life."

 This just blows my mind. Speaking in tongues is like God's secret language.

As the Holy Spirit and God are talking, even though you know nothing about what they are saying, your inner self is being given impressions of things being spoken about. It is building you up, and your faith is built up as well.

Don't be fearful of this gift. It's letting the Holy Spirit intercede for you. Someone told me last week that a problem he had, that was just at a standstill, at a dead end with no hope of success, was suddenly worked out. While he was having his quiet time with the Lord, he marveled about that, and he heard his spirit say that every time he prayed in the spirit, he was asking for help for this. God was just doing what the Holy Spirit and He were talking about. Keep that in mind. God may be smoothing the road ahead with this unknown language spoken through your lips.

Here is my experience. I had the gift of tongues for years but rarely used it for I didn't really understand it. I was challenged to speak in tongues at least three hours during the course of the day. It took a while to build up to that, and seriously, I felt very lonely at first. I was talking but not understanding. However, my inner self was getting it, I guess, for I soon found hours passing and really enjoying this strange time with God.

Evidently the talk was about me writing my first book, for suddenly I was at a conference, saying yes, I would write a book. Even though I only had a title when I said that, the whole book was done in less than two weeks and published a month later. The second day out, it had made the Amazon bestseller list, and I had no idea what it said until I read the finished copy. I know that sounds strange, but I was underlining things in my own book that were from God. They were really God-given nuggets that I didn't come up with. They were prophetic words, and though written in 2016, now in 2017, people are saying what I had written in my book, exact things God had described to me. That had to be the Holy Spirit and God talking this through for this to have happened, for me to write a prophetic book.

The gift of tongues is a wonderful gift, and those who don't understand it will try to deny it even exists today. They are so missing out on a blessing from God.

"And to still another the interpretation of tongues."

Interpretation of tongues and speaking in tongues are the two gifts that interest me the most. Wouldn't it be incredible to be able to start speaking in a different language, much less the language of God? Then, to be able to interpret everything the person's saying without even knowing what they are saying; that's amazing

Interpretation of tongues is not needed if you are alone and the Holy Spirit is speaking through you. The gift of interpretation of tongues is only needed in a group if someone starts speaking out in tongues. Then there should be an interpretation. It most likely is a prophetic word for the group. You can ask for the gift of interpretation.

"So, when you pray in your private prayer language, don't hoard the experience for yourself. Pray for the insight and ability to bring others into that intimacy. If I pray in tongues, my spirit prays but my mind lies fallow, and all that intelligence is wasted. So what's the solution? The answer is simple enough. Do both. I should be spiritually free and expressive as I pray, but I should also be thoughtful and mindful as I pray. I should sing with my spirit, and sing with my mind. If you give a blessing using your private prayer language, which no one else understands, how can some outsider who has just shown up and has no idea what's going on know when to say 'Amen'? Your blessing might be beautiful, but you have very effectively cut that person out of it" (1 Corinthians 14:14–17 The Message).

This gift of an interpretation is not often needed, but you can see the importance of having this gift if it's needed. I have never been anywhere where this gift was needed, so I have not seen this gift in use.

Moving on to Another Book for More Gifts

Another passage of scripture that lets us know about other gifts of the Holy Spirit is found in Ephesians 4:11. Let's look at that, and I will continue describing the gifts mentioned here. This will be from The Message Translation:

"But that doesn't mean you should all look and speak and act the same. Out of the generosity of Christ, each of us is given his own gift. The text for this is,

"He climbed the high mountain,

"He captured the enemy and seized the booty,

"He handed it all out in gifts to the people.

"Is it not true that the One who climbed up also climbed down, down to the valley of earth? And the One who climbed down is the One who climbed back up, up to highest heaven. He handed out gifts above and below, filled heaven with his gifts, filled earth with his gifts. He handed out gifts of apostle, prophet, evangelist, and pastor-teacher to train Christ's followers in skilled servant work, working within Christ's body, the church, until we're all moving rhythmically and easily with each other, efficient and graceful in response to God's Son, fully mature adults, fully developed within and without, fully alive like Christ" (Ephesians 4:11–13).

"He handed out gifts of apostle."

An apostle is one who is sent out to the far corners of the world to start churches. The modern-day term is a missionary. Young and old are receiving this gift.

He handed out gifts of prophet, which we have already talked about.

"He handed out gifts of evangelist."

An evangelist is someone who travels from place to place, preaching the gospel and inviting people to accept Jesus as their personal Savior. The most well-known evangelist in our day is Billy Graham. He has traveled from place to place, filling stadiums with people hungry to hear him preach. Millions have come to know the Lord as their personal Savior because of Billy Graham's gift of evangelism and his obedience to follow the leading of the Lord. According to his staff, more than 3.2 million people have responded to the invitation at Billy Graham Crusades to accept Jesus Christ as their personal Savior. I worked at one of Billy Graham's crusades. It was when he was in San Antonio, Texas, and I was trained by his staff before the crusade to be one of the counselors there for any who came down once Dr. Graham gave the invitation. We gave them gifts, things they needed as a new Christian, and followed up with them in the next few months to make sure they were growing in the Lord. It was quite an experience to be part of Dr. Graham's team. Greg Laurie is a younger pastor/evangelist. He has preached to people all over the world, filling stadiums and overflow rooms, leading many, many thousands to the Lord each year. Greg Laurie comes to our church as a guest preacher, and he in fact was here at our church today.

I have high respect for people who have this gift of evangelism. I think they are so brave to be able to just tell others what they believe, without fear. I know that is something that I am not brave enough to do. So when I see someone like my Bible teacher I had in the fifth grade who can just go up to a stranger and tell them about Jesus, I'm very amazed.

"He handed out gifts of pastor-teacher."

Pastors care for their people who are in their church. They pray for them and want them to live to the fullness of Christ. Pastors with the gift of teaching want the people under them to fully understand each lesson and apply it to their lives. They have the gift from the Holy Spirit to do wonderful lessons, time after time.

One of the most gifted teachers I know is Dr. Jarrett Stephens, one of the pastors at my church. Dr. Stephens was kind enough to let me use his testimony of his calling to the ministry, and you will find that in the back of this book. He has the well-developed gift to take any subject and allow complete understanding of why we need to apply it, to avoid it, or to search for it. Dr. Stephens is a young man, but he also has the gift of caring that pastors have. He lets you know that he has time for you, he is there to help you, and he will help you to the best of his ability. What an honor to know Dr. Stephens.

Romans Is the Last Book Mentioning Gifts

The last passage we are going to look at is Romans 12:6–8.

"We have different gifts, according to the grace given to each of us. If your gift is prophesying, then prophesy in accordance with your faith; if it is serving, then serve; if it is teaching, then teach; if it is to encourage, then give encouragement; if it is giving, then give generously; if it is to lead, do it diligently; if it is to show mercy, do it cheerfully" (Romans 12:6–8 NIV).

"If it is serving, then serve."

Those with the gift of service see a need and get to work on it. They are the ones you see staying after a party and getting the dishes done or putting away the chairs. They would rather take care of the need themselves than delegate the task, for they delight in getting short-term projects done. They never seem to tire when a short-term need is in front of them. They meet the needs quickly, freeing others to achieve other things. They enjoy being around people and are the ones to remember the details of their lives, such as their children's name, ages, likes, and dislikes. This is a God-given part of their gifting, which helps them better serve.

If you have this gift, you must avoid not being under the influence of the Holy Spirit. Then this gift turns into a pity party, feeling you have to do all the work, focusing on only yourself and finally giving up. Under the influence of the Holy Spirit, the gift of serving brings delight to people, and they do like to receive approval and recognition for seeing the need and quickly taking care it. Remember that, and let them know how much they are appreciated.

"If it is teaching, then teach."

Those with the teaching gift have the God-given ability to study the Word of God and explain it in a way that others can apply to their lives. Jesus was great at everything, and we know He is a great teacher. He would take a truth and explain it in a parable so it could be applied in that person's life. I went to college to earn a degree in teaching, but this gift of teaching is not learned in college. It is a God-given ability to understand the Bible clearly and teach how it can be walked out in life. Though we looked at the pastor-teacher, this gift of teaching is not only given to pastors. This is a gift that can be given to anyone. I saw a video and posted it on my Facebook page of a little girl teaching a room full of adults. She was using no notes, teaching with delight on how to be a funnel for God's blessings and powers, and clearly under the anointing of the Holy Spirit. The little girl, probably eight or nine years old, was God's instrument.

"If it is the gift of encourage, then encouragement."

Barnabas is a wonderful biblical example of someone with the gift of encouragement. He was always calling others to his side to encourage them to keep their hope in God. If they needed help, he was there. If they were feeling down, he encouraged them by showing them how to be an instrument for Christ with their lives. You can read about Barnabas in Acts. One with this gift sees something good in others and immediately lets them know. It is always good to hear an encouraging word. They are the ones to bring hope to those in despair.

You can spot an encourager anywhere. They are so quick to say an encouraging word to you just because they are thinking in the positive and want to tell you those good thoughts. That has shown up as one of my gifts, but I have never seen a more encouraging person than Anne Swartout. Anne and I were connected by a lot of moves by God to meet at a conference. Anne is from Connecticut, and I'm from Texas. The CEO of the conference is from Holland, and Anne and I both found ourselves at this Christian conference with people from all over the world. We got to be known as "the Anne and Ann team."

This conference was where the challenge went out to write a book, and both Anne and I said yes. Anne and I even meeting was a totally divine connection. I don't play chess, but it seemed like a series of chess moves. This person was moved there, that person was moved over here, another person was unable to go so got knocked off the board, one person didn't answer emails so no one knew where she should go, so Anne and I were put together as roommates at the crowded hotel. We laugh about all God had to do to connect us.

Anne is the most encouraging person I have ever met, and I am so blessed to have her as a friend. For almost two years, we have been cohosts on the Holy Spirit Global Intercessor Team Healing Room. Technology lets us be in two different states and lead this webinar twice a week. Anne is constantly encouraging me about this book, sensing I need that encouragement since it has been so slow to get finished. She has no idea how these speed bumps that I have hit have so discouraged me. Anne is also one of my endorsers. Oh, you will know when you have met someone with the well-honed gift of encouragement. You will be so blessed.

 I had a friend who was an encourager. She always made me feel smart and beautiful. That is a weird thing to say today, because the cool thing is to smack talk and bring others down as you build yourself up. Even friends do this to each other. In fact, in the world we live today, kids from even first grade and up have hardened and learn mean comebacks and burning words just to survive school. So when you meet an encourager, you'll know it. They are like a bright light in this world that is slowly getting darker. Help that encourager and learn from them, and don't fall in the ways of the world. Take me, for example. At school, they call me "Twinkle" and make fun of me because I don't watch PG-13 movies or know how to smack talk. My teachers and friends tell me they know me as one of the happiest people on earth. Even if it's not cool, be an encourager. Be the happiest, friendliest person people know. Let's be the generation that makes being a nice person normal and cool.

It sounds as if you also have the gift of encourager, Carlisle. That would be wonderful if your generation changed things around and students quit hurting each other with unkind words. I hope they listen to you.

That's the last of the mentioned gifts.

Wait, What about the Gift of Intercession?

Isn't that interesting? There is no mention of intercession being a gift in any of those passages, but so many of us say it's one of our gifts. There are some of us who have the supernatural love to pray for others. The desire to pray for others seems to be an outpouring from another gift, from many of the other gifts. Let's consider this.

Faith. How does intercession entwine with the gift of faith?

You have the gift of faith, and you have such a confidence that

God can help this person, so you naturally want to intercede for them, and so you pray for them until you see the answer come.

Encouragement. How does intercession entwine with the gift of encouragement?

You are such a positive person, and if people need God to move on a situation that has discouraged them, you naturally want to intercede for them and so pray until there is an answer.

Pastor. How does intercession entwine with the gift of pastoring?

Pastors pray for their flock, and their flock has many needs. A pastor has the supernatural ability to pray for these needs, delighting when God provides.

Healing. How does intercession entwine with the gift of healing?

If you have the gift of healing, you have a firm grip on the power of God to heal; therefore, it is amazingly easy to pray for that person to be healed and whole.

Are you seeing what I mean? It is a supernatural ability to stand in the gap and pray for a touch from God for the person in need. It is supernatural, not hard to do, not a burden, though I have known some intercessors who awaken in the night and travail in prayer until they are released from a burden they were feeling for a person. I know what that is like. Many years ago, I had a sudden knowing I was to pray for a friend. She is gone now, having died of natural causes. This was in the 1980s; I knew I had to pray for her but had no idea what was going on in her house. The enemy didn't want me to pray, and I developed a terrible migraine, but I continued to pray. I sensed the need was great. After about two hours, the burden lifted, and I was able to go to sleep.

That next morning, I called to ask what was going on last night, for God had me praying for those two hours for her. I was shocked when she told me that she and her husband were going to kill themselves. They had closed the garage door and turned the car on, but they had then turned it off. Again, they turned the car on in that closed garage, and again they had turned it off. This had gone on for two hours, and finally they decided to go in, have dinner, and go to bed. My goodness. If you ever get the urging to pray for someone, do it.

I think intercession is one of my gifts. When I pray for someone, it is easy for me to do. When I pray to God, often I end up in tears because of what I have realized while talking to Him. I often wish I could write down what is flowing out of me, because it is all so amazing. So far, I have never remembered enough to write it down. It is like just God's and my secret conversations.

You can ask God for all these gifts; as a Christian, the Holy Spirit will certainly give some to you. As God gives you things to do, you will be gifted by the Holy Spirit to enable you to accomplish it. We must not waste our gifts but develop them to the fullest to help the body of Christ. That is what they are for.

Chapter 14

What We Learn from Sheep

Let me tell you my firsthand experience with sheep. It was in 1981, and Bob was stationed at Ramstein Air Force Base in Germany. That first year there, we lived off base in a little German village called Weltersbach. Our house was on a cul-de-sac, and all the land past that was fields.

One day, I was washing the dishes and glanced out the kitchen window. What a surprise to see an area of grass next to the house across the street, full of sheep. That rather large flock, seventy-five to one hundred of them, were happily grazing on that fresh green grass. Suddenly I saw our dog running over to them, and I was horrified to see what happened next.

The first sheep that saw our German shepherd dog running toward them panicked and ran. The entire flock was now in a panic, and off they all went down the street. Our quick-acting German shepherd, who had never seen sheep in her life, instinctively knew what to do. Snickers ran, circling the sheep until they stopped, turned around, gathered back on the grass, and stood still.

Now the sheepdog, who was there all the time on duty, had a thing or two to tell Snickers, and that was said and done in a minute. It probably went something like this: "These are my sheep, my responsibility, and I never want to see you near them again." I have no idea where the shepherd himself had gone, but he was there when I first spotted the sheep.

Snickers came in the house, and being a dog that liked to tell stories, told me all about it, in her language. I was so proud of Snickers knowing what to do to save those sheep but very concerned about what could have happened had she not known what to do. Apparently, the shepherd had no idea what all had gone on while he was away, for I never heard or saw him again.

I did learn this from watching those sheep: one sheep can cause an entire flock to run, without thinking, right into danger. Do we panic like that when one person reacts in fear?

Why am I talking about sheep, anyway? God compares us to sheep in the Bible:

"Know that the LORD, he is God!
It is he who made us, and we are his;
we are his people, and the sheep of his pasture" (Psalm 100:3 English Standard Version [ESV]).

This verse says that we belong to God. That means God will protect us, His children, His sheep.

Sheep are the most mentioned animal in the Bible, and we Christians are the Lord's sheep. God is our shepherd and will guide us; there are so many Scriptures that tell us that.

The 23rd Psalm is the first whole chapter I memorized as a very little girl. Let's look at the first three verses:

"The LORD is my shepherd; I shall not want.
He makes me lie down in green pastures: he leads me beside the still waters.
He restores my soul: he leads me in the paths of righteousness for his name's sake" (Psalm 23:1–3 ESV).

We, like the sheep in these verses, need God to do this for us. It is a fact we need God to take care of us and protect us.

As I said, I don't know where that shepherd went across the street, but he left them in green pastures with a well-trained sheepdog, unaware of our wannabe sheepdog.

The Lord is our shepherd, and He is very aware of all the dangers around. We are His sheep. Let's look at more verses:

"But we your people, the sheep of your pasture,
will give thanks to you forever;
from generation to generation we will recount your praise" (Psalm 79:13 ESV).

We, God's people, the sheep of His pasture, give thanks to God for taking care of us. We taught our children to give God praise, for He takes care of us, and now teach our children's children to do the same.

These other scriptures that I'm going to show you tell us what the shepherd has to watch for as he tends the sheep. Our shepherd is very alert to these things. What do sheep teach us? Some good things and some bad examples:

"I have strayed like a lost sheep.
Seek your servant,
for I have not forgotten your commands" (Psalm 119:176 NIV).

"We all, like sheep, have gone astray,
each of us has turned to our own way;

and the LORD has laid on him
the iniquity of us all" (Isaiah 53:6 NIV).
When we wander like sheep, God, like the good shepherd, will go after us, making sure we are okay.

We all have wandered off, away from the right path we were placed on. Thankfully, our shepherd does come to look for us. The shepherd will leave all his other sheep to go look for that one, and perhaps that is what the shepherd in Germany was doing. He may have counted and knew one was missing. Have you seen that picture in church lessons of Jesus carrying one little sheep back to the flock on His shoulders?

Sheep stray, looking for that next best blade of grass, not aware of how far they have wandered. We do the same, not looking for the next blade of grass to eat, but looking for something the world has dangled like a carrot in front of us. Off we go to try to catch it, unaware of the dangerous path we are on.

Why is it dangerous for sheep to wander off? Many reasons:

1) They are out of the sight of the shepherd.
2) The sheep may be on uneven ground and roll over on his back.
3) There may be a predator just looking for a stray sheep to devour.
4) They are out of the sound of the shepherd's voice.

We will take a look at each of those four. Perhaps we will learn something that relates to us.

We have protection; we learned from studying Psalm 91 in a previous chapter that we are safe in the shadow of the Most High. We feel safe when we are right there with our shepherd watching over us. The Holy Spirit in us takes away the fear.

"For God hath not given us the spirit of fear; but of power, and of love, and of a sound mind" (2 Timothy 1:7 KJV).

A sound mind is a mind at rest, at peace about the future. Sheep don't have to worry about the dangers of the night with their shepherd watching over them. If they have wandered away, there is no protection. Let's learn from sheep to not wander away from the protection of our Father's outstretched arms.

Read Psalm 91:1–6 in The Message Translation:
"You who sit down in the High God's presence,
spend the night in Shaddai's shadow,
Say this: 'GOD, you're my refuge.
I trust in you and I'm safe!'
That's right—he rescues you from hidden traps,
shields you from deadly hazards.
His huge outstretched arms protect you—
under them you're perfectly safe;
his arms fend off all harm.
Fear nothing—not wild wolves in the night,
not flying arrows in the day."

Sheep looking up from their grazing to see their shepherd right there must feel peace as well, knowing he will chase away predators. However, concentrating only on the next blade of grass, leaving the area, and then realizing that the shepherd is no longer in sight must bring on a rush of fear in that sheep.

Let's look at point number two, at the sheep that wandered now being on uneven ground. What is the problem there? First of all, a shepherd looks for good pasture land that is a large area with plenty of green grass and low plants for the sheep to eat. That area across from where we were living in Germany never reminded me of pasture land. It definitely had lush green grass, but it was just a small side yard next to a house. That's exactly what it was. Suddenly, every inch of it was filled with the flock of sheep eating that lush green grass, unaware of a strange, curious dog nearby. I wish you could have been looking out my kitchen window with me to see that sight.

If you are a city person like me, you would have barely recovered from seeing the sight of that flock of sheep in your neighborhood, when you would have realized our dog was trotting across the street to have a look. Everything unfolded in the next few minutes: the quiet flock of sheep now frantically rushing into the street and starting down the hill toward a very busy road. The next sight was our dog circling the sheep two or three times, making them stop and head back to the grass. This was over in less than five minutes, and it appeared all the sheep were fine. I'm so thankful for the God-given instincts in our German shepherd, her knowing what to do. I'm so thankful that the sheep didn't fall on the uneven part where the curb was or lose their balance as they ran down the hilly street. Now that I think about all this, I have a lot to praise God about, don't I? We could have been charged for the lost flock if it had gone a different way. (By the way, this wonderful German shepherd of ours lived to be eighteen, and I have told stories about her in my first two books. This wonderful dog helped raise our children.)

What happens when sheep are on uneven ground? I am sure you have seen that wonderful picture of Jesus with the lost lamb that had been found being carried back to the flock. That picture must be in every church's Sunday school area, and it depicts the Parable of the Lost Sheep, one of the parables of Jesus. It appears in Matthew 18:12–14 and Luke 15:3–7. It is about a shepherd who leaves his flock of ninety-nine sheep in order to find the one that is lost. Why is it so important that a shepherd leave ninety-nine sheep to go search for the one that was lost? That's because it quite often is a matter of life and death. The Bible tells us that we, like sheep, have gone astray, each to his own way. When a lamb goes off on its own, it can get in trouble. The land can get rough, causing it to tumble over on its back. The problem when any sheep falls and ends up on its back is that it can die because it can't get back up. It is lying there helpless. Gases build up in its body, cutting off circulation to its extremities. If it's hot, it only can live a few hours. That is why shepherds keep careful count of their flock and race off if one is missing. When the shepherd finds them, hopefully it is in time, and they help them to their side. Their legs are so wobbly that if they can carry it, it will be carried back to the rest of the flock. If it is too heavy to lift, they will massage the sheep's legs to get the circulation back and lead them back.

How often does Jesus have to go searching for us, to bring us back to where we should be? Are we lost and lying helpless, hoping the vultures or wild animals don't find us? Are we unaware we have even strayed? Isaiah 53:6 tells us we are all like sheep who have gone astray. If we are still alive, we were found in time and brought back to safety. It's the better deal all around to be where we are supposed to be. God wants to find us before we get on rough, uneven ground and fall, before we fall into a trap set by the enemy. It's better to be there beside Him, content in the safety of His reach, to be able to hear His voice and keep our focus on Him.

John 10:27 tells us the sheep know their master's voice, hear him, and they follow him. It also says that the shepherd knows them. A friend of mine returned from Israel with a wonderful story about this. An old shepherd living over in Israel told her that when the lambs are born, he makes it a point to spend fifteen minutes at a time, several times a day, giving it his individual attention. This goes on for months. He will pet it, talk to it, and in this way, the little lamb gets used to hearing his voice. Likewise, the shepherd gets to know each little lamb, its personality, and calls it by name. I really love this story and am glad it was told to me in such a timely manner that I can use it in this chapter. Don't you think the little lamb takes on the gentleness of the shepherd who shows his love to that lamb? Just by giving that little lamb that much individual attention three or four times a day makes it realize it is indeed loved and cared for.

 That is true a sheep knows its master's voice. I watched a video on this. In the video, a random person would come to a flock of sheep and say the same thing the shepherd would. When the random person did it, the sheep didn't even look up. Two or three different people tried calling the sheep like this. When the

shepherd called them, every one of the sheep looked up and started walking to their shepherd. It was amazing to see.

In biblical times, it was really important for sheep to know their master's voice, for many shepherds would bring their sheep to one pasture and let them graze together. When it was time to leave, each shepherd would call his flock, and only his sheep would separate and follow their shepherd.

We are God's children, and God is the one who compares us to sheep. God is able to spend as much time with us as we allow Him. He is not limited in what He can do, as the shepherd in Israel is, and God loves us so much more than we can even imagine. God wants us to spend time with Him, to know His voice when He calls, and realize that the one who loves us the most wants to visit with us, has something special to say to us. No wonder God wants to let the little children come to Him, for as the shepherd in Israel started teaching his flock as lambs, God wants to start teaching us as infants. I feel loved being compared to sheep, for the good shepherds watching over them are amazing. Our good shepherd is infinitely more awesome and amazing. I'm glad we are His sheep.

Testimonies

God Interacting with Children and Young Teens

God often goes to great lengths to get us to know things. This, indeed, is one of those times. It delights me whenever I think about it. I opened my e-mail, and there was a blog on one of the inspirational blog posts to which I subscribe. As I read the blog that morning, it really spoke to me, but that wasn't what I wanted to tell you. I was led to write Dana Jarvis, the author of the blog, and tell her what an encouragement she was to me. I mentioned that I was writing this book and asked her if I could talk to her about stories she had about children and faith. Dana wrote back that she would love to do that. I had no idea she even had a testimony, but she had some that involved her own son. (No wonder God led me to ask her.) However, the story gets better. God is a God of details, and I learned later that Dana has a ministry with quite a following. It is called the Hezekiah Wall Ministry. I looked it up and clicked on the "About" link to learn more. This is what came up:

"Hezekiah's Wall Ministry is to Equip, Empower, Encourage, And Raise Up the Sons and Daughters of God for such a time as this!"

God is quite amazing knowing all the little details and weaving His children's lives together. He is so much fun.

In this first story, Dana gives us a perfect example of God touching a small child:

"I had raised up my son Dylan in church, and by the age of six, he would get up and sing songs that I taught him. That is, what he could remember of them.

"One day I heard him shouting, and he was standing on a small foot bridge that led across a stream, just standing there preaching. You could make out most of the words, especially words like 'Praise God.' I saw such fire in my little boy. He acted as if he was preaching to a congregation as he looked in front of him. He kept moving his hands and preaching at the top of his voice, which was almost similar to how our pastor at the time sounded when he got fired up in his sermons. That was one very fond memory I will never forget."

Dana's next story occurred when Dylan was eighteen, and this will encourage you to believe that angels are on earth to assist us:

"When Dylan was eighteen, he went out with a group of friends one night. It was a wintry night, and the driver lost control of the car, and it left the road. Well, that very night, before this happened, I was getting ready for bed, and the Lord spoke to me and said, "Pray for Dylan." I had such a feeling overwhelm me that I hit my knees and prayed for him before lying down.

"It was about 10:30 when my dad called and told me that Dylan had been in an accident. My heart just hit the floor. Dylan was okay.

"Later, Dylan shared with me what he encountered during the accident. Some of what Dylan told me, I already knew. You see after that call from my dad, God immediately showed me in a vision what happened and confirmed it word for word, long before Dylan told me.

"Dylan said once they left the road, he saw everything flash before him. He saw me, my mom, and so many others, and he thought he would not make it out alive. They struck a tree, turning the car on its side. His two friends in the front seat were killed instantly, but Dylan was in the back seat. His leg was caught under the seat, and he could not get free. But then, he said, suddenly his leg just lifted, and he climbed out the window. Seeking help, he made his way to the top of the hill and fell to the ground but then was able to get back up. He saw a bright light appear in front of him, and it started to move, so he followed it. He followed it until it finally disappeared, and when it disappeared, there was a house right in front of him.

"In my vision before Dylan shared the story with me, God showed me my son trapped in that car and the angel of the Lord freeing his legs. He showed me one angel on each side of Dylan escorting him up the hill to the road. I saw Dylan fall down, but they each took one arm and lifted him back up, leading him safely to the nearby house for help. I know that I know God saved my son that night, and we have this testimony left to share about it. Sadly, he did lose two of his friends in the accident, but I praise God for saving my son. I always love to share this testimony of God's goodness and saving hand."

Dana Jarvis

Hezekiah's Wall Ministry

Dylan is twenty-four now, married, and works in a job helping people with mental and physical handicaps. He's in a job that many of us couldn't do, and this is clearly part of what God has for him. Dana is confident of God's leading in Dylan's life and is claiming that her son will step into his full potential as he focuses on God. Dana stands on Proverbs 22:6 KJV: "Train up a child in the way he should go: and when he is old, he will not depart from it."

Dana said that she is amazed that God told me to contact her. Well, Dana, God truly did. Indeed, He has a plan. The anointing was so strong that I was nearly knocked off my chair when I typed these words.

Watch the children. In the eyes of a child, God can do anything. So whatever it is that is going on, there is no need for worry if you have turned it over to God.

Here is another beautiful testimony showing that a child really knows God's there to help her. I asked Michele if she could give an example of how she knew, but she could only say again, "God was just always there." I shared Michele and Melvin's testimony of their encounter with a rattlesnake and their little dog, Raja. This is from my friend, Michele Pillay:

God's Hand on My Life
by Michele Grace Pillay

God is a masterful Creator and a loving Father who has a plan and purpose for our lives before we are ever in our mother's womb, before our parents even thought of wanting to have a child. Even before the beginning of time, God knew us. He saw our unformed beings and had written out all our days even before He created us, before He fashioned us in our mother's womb. His love for us is never ending, and truly no one can love us like He can, for He created us.

When God formed me, He chose my eye color, my hair color, and knew what my smile would be like. He knew how tall I would become and even knew the number of the hairs on my head.

Even before I was born, He had a beautiful story written out for me. He had a purpose, a plan, a destiny, and a special calling for me because He chose me. God knew the woman I would grow up to be and that I would fulfill the purpose He laid before me.

And yes, I am the woman He knew I would be, and yes, my passion and desire is to daily walk closer to the Lord and to fulfill every plan, purpose, and destiny He has set before me. Now, this does not mean that my life has been perfect and that I do not have struggles and challenges, because I do.

From the time I was just an infant, I experienced many medical challenges. I spent the first nine weeks of my life in the hospital. But the Lord was with me as an infant, as a child, as a teen, and He is with me as an adult. God is with me and has walked with me every step of my journey, and I know that His hand has been on my life all along.

At the tender age of five, I gave my heart to Jesus Christ, and I have never looked back. I invited Him into my heart and asked Him to guide my every footstep and to light my way, and He has done just that.

In the Word of God, He says, "I will never leave you, nor forsake you" (Hebrews 13:5), and the Lord has been faithful to keep the promise of this scripture in my life. Now, there were times in the midst of challenges in my life that I walked away from God, but oh, He is so faithful, and He was waiting for me every time I ran back to Him. You see, He never left me. He never took His hand off of my life. I was the one who stepped away from Him, but even when I was a backslider, He was right there carrying me, for He is a good, good Father.

Now, not always does God show Himself to us in the natural, but I believe that He does send His angels to watch over us. After I was married, the Lord revealed to Melvin that during those nine weeks I spent in the hospital, and many hours alone as my parents had to go to work, the Lord sent two angels to my bedside to sing over me and comfort me. And again later in life, He sent those same two angels to my bedside when I was very ill.

You see, dear friends, if we will just open our hearts to the Lord and ask Him to come, He will guide us, He will lead us, and He will place His hand on our lives. We don't have to walk through life alone; we have a loving heavenly Father who wants to walk with us, and oh, what a beautiful story He has written for us, if we will only surrender to Him.

Dear friends, God is not a respecter of persons, and so I am confident that He has a plan, purpose, and destiny for you to walk into and fulfill.

The Lord has been so faithful to me, and He has made something beautiful of my life. Through all my challenges, He has a made a beautiful testimony for His glory, and I believe that He wants the same for you. Your story may be different from mine, and your struggles may be different from mine, but what we have in common is a great God who wants to make something beautiful of your life and wants to make a beautiful testimony for His glory. Amen.

Michele Grace Pillay
Evangelist, World Voice of Hope Foundation

This next testimony I am so pleased to be able to share is from Dr. Jarrett Stephens, an extremely gifted teaching pastor at Prestonwood Baptist Church in Plano, Texas. This is our home church, and woven through sermons, I've heard Dr. Stephens tell of how God touched his heart as a boy. Carlisle and I met with him, and I asked Dr. Stephens if we could use his testimony in our book. He agreed.

Dr. Stephens graduated from Ouachita Baptist University with a bachelor of arts in biblical studies and psychology. He received his master of divinity from Southwestern Baptist Theological Seminary and his doctorate of ministry from Liberty Theological Seminary in 2012. He and his wife, Debbie, have four daughters; the oldest one is Carlisle's age.

Dr. Stephens told the following story to Carlisle and me:

"I was raised in a church. Mom and Dad didn't just drop me off at church; they led me to church. One of my earliest memories is singing in the choir with Dad. Remember that song, 'Joy, Joy, Joy, Joy, Down in My Heart'? I loved church; there was never a time when I didn't want to go. I had a great foundation."

Turning to Carlisle, Dr. Stephens continued, "I was in a small group in sixth grade, your age, Carlisle, and I remember hearing the pastor talk. It was like yesterday. I was eleven years old, and it was August 3, 1989. The pastor was giving a chalk talk. There was a boat and the waves, you could tell, were rough. He put a black light on it, and a lighthouse appeared. There was the face of Jesus, letting us know Christ is always watching out for us. Shortly after that small group, the Spirit of the Lord prompted me, and I accepted Christ as my personal Savior.

"My goal was to play college football and pursue a coaching career. I was involved with Fellowship of Christian Athletes and was asked to give the devotion at fifth quarter. (Fifth quarter was after the game and time with the Lord.) I gave that devotional, and that solidified the call on my life. I was seventeen years old, and it was like being hit by a bolt of lightning. My parents saw this gifting in me to teach, and they encouraged me all the way."

Dr. Jarrett Stephens
Teaching Pastor
Prestonwood Baptist Church, Plano, Texas

Remember Nubia's son, Miquel, who said no so boldly that she knew it came straight from God through her son? Nubia became my Christian mentor, very much allowing me to be where I am now in my walk with my Lord.

Well, Miquel grew up, is serving in the Navy, and is married with an almost three-year-old daughter. His daughter, Nathalia, is already gifted in healing and understands praying in the power of the name of Jesus.

I have permission to share the following two testimonies about Miquel's daughter, Nathalia:

My friend and Christian mentor, Nubia, now lives with her son and his wife, and takes care of Nathalia, as both parents work. Every day, Nubia and little Nathalia go for a walk. One day, two dogs somehow got out of a house they passed, ran barking to the fence, and crawled under the gate. Nubia picked her granddaughter up and told her not to move. Without a moment's hesitation, little Nathalia started to pray, "Help us in the name of Jesus." They were fine. The dogs stopped jumping on them, began circling around them, and then walked back toward their house. Nubia was amazed at her granddaughter's quick thinking and the perfect solution for their situation: a quick prayer.

A few weeks ago, Nubia got a papercut under her fingernail. It hurt, as paper cuts always do, but she didn't think anything about it. However, a few days later, it was very infected and painful. After over a week, it was still swollen and infected.

She said to Miquel, "Look at this. I guess I will have to go to the doctor."

Nathalia was sitting on her daddy's lap, and Miquel said, "Why don't you pray for your grandmother, Nathalia?"

Nubia said that she prayed the sweetest prayer, ending it with "In Jesus's name."

Nubia thought it was sweet but didn't realize the power of a child's prayer. The next morning, the swelling had gone down, and the pain had lessened. The second day after the prayer, there was no pain and no sign of infection. God honored the faith of a little girl, who was only two years old at the time.

Told to Ann Noble by Nubia Barrios

Permission to share given by Miquel Barrios

Spring Branch, Texas

Conclusion

 Through this book, I have learned things about myself and about God. It has been so amazing to start writing and then sometimes even start crying after reading what I had written. Those words and thoughts could only have come from the Holy Spirit.

I just want to thank my incredible Grammy for giving me the opportunity to be a part of this with her. She is an amazing godly person.

Thank you, Carlisle, for praying this book through with me. It indeed took a lot of prayer. We both learned a lot from the Holy Spirit, that He is so ready to reveal Himself to us, to teach and guide us. Separately, we were taught by Him, though united in what we needed to know, and we both were overwhelmed to the point of tears, realizing that He was right there, doing just that.

Never despise small beginnings. It starts with just a mustard seed of faith.

Bless you, children, for showing us adults how to think like you do.

Thank you for letting God speak to you and through you to us. Thank you.

Endnotes

Chapter 2
Eleven Visions Mentioned in the Bible

1. "He had a dream in which he saw a stairway resting on the earth, with its top reaching to heaven, and the angels of God were ascending and descending on it. There above it stood the LORD, and he said: 'I am the LORD, the God of your father Abraham and the God of Isaac. I will give you and your descendants the land on which you are lying'" (Genesis 28:12–13 NIV).
2. "Moses and Aaron, Nadab and Abihu, and the seventy elders of Israel went up and saw the God of Israel. Under his feet was something like a pavement made of lapis lazuli, as bright blue as the sky" (Exodus 24:9–10 NIV).
3. "Then I will remove my hand and you will see my back; but my face must not be seen" (Exodus 33:23 NIV)
4. "Micaiah continued, 'Therefore hear the word of the LORD: I saw the LORD sitting on his throne with all the multitudes of heaven standing on his right and on his left'" (2 Chronicles 18:18 NIV).
5. "In my vision at night I looked, and there before me was one like a son of man, coming with the clouds of heaven. He approached the Ancient of Days and was led into his presence" (Daniel 7:13 NIV).
6. "During the night Paul had a vision of a man of Macedonia standing and begging him, 'Come over to Macedonia and help us.' After Paul had seen the vision, we got ready at once to leave for Macedonia, concluding that God had called us to preach the gospel to them" (Acts 16:9–10 NIV).

7. "But [they] didn't find his body. They came and told us that they had seen a vision of angels, who said he was alive" (Luke 24:23 NIV).

8. "I, Daniel, was the only one who saw the vision; those who were with me did not see it, but such terror overwhelmed them that they fled and hid themselves" (Daniel 10:7 NIV).

9. "Then the Lord replied,
   'Write down the revelation
   and make it plain on tablets
   so that a herald may run with it.
   For the revelation awaits an appointed time;
   it speaks of the end
   and will not prove false.
   Though it linger, wait for it;
   it will certainly surely come'" (Habakuk 2:2–3 NIV).

10. "And afterward,
    I will pour out my Spirit on all people.
    Your sons and daughters will prophesy,
    your old men will dream dreams,
    your young men will see visions.
    Even on my servants, both men and women,
    I will pour out my Spirit in those days" (Joel 2:28–29 NIV).

11. "I know a man in Christ who fourteen years ago was caught up to the third heaven. Whether it was in the body or out of the body I do not know—God knows" (2 Corinthians 12:2 NIV).

Chapter 8
Twenty-Three Verses to Fight Apathy or Indifference to God

1. "There is much we could say about this, but it is hard to make you understand. It is because you do not want to hear well. By now you should be teachers. Instead, you need someone to teach you again the first things you need to

know from God's Word. You still need milk instead of solid food" (Hebrews 5:11–12 NLV).

2. "We are not of those people who turn back and are lost. Instead, we have faith to be saved from the punishment of sin" (Hebrews 10:39 NLV).

3. "Be sure you listen to the One Who is speaking to you. The Jews did not obey when God's Law was given to them on earth. They did not go free. They were punished. We will be punished more if we do not listen to God as He speaks from heaven" (Hebrews 12:25 NLV).

4. "There is One Who can keep you from falling and can bring you before Himself free from all sin. He can give you great joy as you stand before Him in His shining-greatness" (Jude 1:24 NLV).

5. "If you think it is wrong to serve the Lord, choose today whom you will serve. Choose the gods your fathers worshiped on the other side of the river, or choose the gods of the Amorites in land you are living. But as for me and my family, we will serve the Lord" (Joshua 24:15 NLV).

6. "Wake up! Make stronger what you have before it dies. I have not found your work complete in God's sight" (Revelation 3:2 NLV).

7. "I know what you are doing. You are not cold or hot. I wish you were one or the other. But because you are warm, and not hot or cold, I will spit you out of My mouth" (Revelation 3:15–16 NLV).

8. "At that time I will look through Jerusalem with a light and will punish those who take it easy and do not care what happens. They say in their hearts, 'The Lord will not do good or bad.' Their riches will be taken from them and their houses will be laid waste. They will build houses but not live in them. They will plant grape-fields but not drink their wine" (Zephaniah 1:12–13 NLV).

9. "Do not be lazy but always work hard. Work for the Lord with a heart full of love for Him" (Romans 12:11 NLV).

10. "The time will come when people will not listen to the truth. They will look for teachers who will tell them only what they want to hear. They will not listen to the truth. Instead, they will listen to stories made up by men" (2 Timothy 4:3–4 NLV).

11. "This is the last thing I want to say: Be strong with the Lord's strength. Put on the things God gives you to fight with. Then you will not fall into the traps of the devil. Our fight is not with people. It is against the leaders and the powers and the spirits of darkness in this world. It is against the demon world that works in the heavens" (Ephesians 6:10–12 NLV).

12. "Be sure your love is true love. Hate what is sinful. Hold on to whatever is good. Love each other as Christian brothers. Show respect for each other. Do not be lazy but always work hard. Work for the Lord with a heart full of love for Him. Be happy in your hope. Do not give up when trouble comes. Do not let anything stop you from praying. Share what you have with Christian brothers who are in need. Give meals and a place to stay to those who need it" (Romans 12:9–13 NLV).

13. "The path of the lazy man is grown over with thorns, but the path of the faithful is a good road" (Proverbs 15:19 NLV).

14. "Make the best use of your time. These are sinful days" (Ephesians 5:16 NLV).

15. "You do read the Holy Writings. You think you have life that lasts forever just because you read them. They do tell of Me. But you do not want to come to Me so you might have life" (John 5:39–40 NLV).

16. "'Watch and pray so that you will not be tempted. Man's spirit wants to do this, but the body does not have the power to do it.' "Again Jesus went away and prayed saying the same words. He came back and found them sleeping again. Their eyes were heavy. They did not know what to say to Him. He came the third time and said to them, 'Are you still sleeping

and resting? It is enough! Listen, the time has come when the Son of Man will be handed over to sinners'" (Mark 14:38–41 NLV).

17. "If you know what is right to do but you do not do it, you sin" (James 4:17 NLV).

18. "Whatever your hand finds to do, do it with all your strength. For there is no work or planning or learning or wisdom in the place of the dead where you are going" (Ecclesiastes 9:10 NLV).

19. "A man cannot please God unless he has faith. Anyone who comes to God must believe that He is. That one must also know that God gives what is promised to the one who keeps on looking for Him" (Hebrews 11:6 NLV).

20. "He who is lazy in his work is a brother to him who destroys" (Proverbs 18:9 NLV).

21. "A little sleep, a little rest, a little folding of the hands to rest, and your being poor will come as a robber, and your need like a man ready to fight" (Proverbs 24:33–34 NLV).

22. "Do not let yourselves get tired of doing good. If we do not give up, we will get what is coming to us at the right time" (Galatians 6:9 NLV).

23. "They do not care anymore about what is right or wrong. They have turned themselves over to the sinful ways of the world and are always wanting to do every kind of sinful act they can think of" (Ephesians 4:19 NLV).

Chapter 12
Healing Scriptures

"I cry out to the Lord and He heals me" (Psalm 30:2).

"The Lord forgives all my sins and heals all my diseases" (Psalm 103:3).

"He sends His Word and heals me and rescues me from the pit of destruction" (Psalm 107:20).

"I shall not die but live, and shall declare the works and recount the illustrious acts of the Lord" (Psalm 118:17).

"He heals my broken heart and binds up my wounds" (Psalm 147:3).

"I will listen closely to God's Words. I will not let them out of my sight. I will keep them within my heart for they are life for all who find them and health for the whole body" (Proverbs 4:20–22).

"My light shall break forth like the morning, and my healing shall spring forth speedily" (Isaiah 58:8).

"Heal me O Lord and I shall be healed. Save me and I shall be saved, for You are my praise" (Jeremiah 17:14).

"The Lord has declared that He will restore my health and heal my wounds" (Jeremiah 30:17).

"When I am sick, I will call on the elders to pray over me and anoint me with oil in the name of the Lord. And the prayer offered in faith will make me well; the Lord will raise me up" (James 5:14–15).

"He Himself bore my sins in His body on the tree, so that I might die to sins and live for righteousness; by His wounds I have been healed" (1 Peter 2:24).

"I pray that I may enjoy good health and that all may go well with me, even as my soul is getting along well" (3 John 2).

About the Authors

Ann Lynn Noble grew up in Oklahoma City, Oklahoma, and graduated from the University of Oklahoma, earning a BS degree in education. She and Robert Noble met in Denver, Colorado, where Ann moved for her first teaching job and Bob moved to attend the USAF Officer Training School. Ann and Bob celebrated their fifty-second wedding anniversary in August of 2017. They have three grown successful children and three beautiful granddaughters.

As a military wife, Ann saw her husband advance from a second lieutenant to a full colonel. They moved seventeen times, and Ann ended up teaching first through eighth grades, both in public and Christian schools.

Bob left for two yearlong remotes, the first to Vietnam when Ann was two months pregnant with their firstborn. The second remote tour was to Saudi Arabia, leaving Ann and their three children, ages five through ten. They traveled Europe when stationed in Germany from 1981 to 1984. Now living in the Dallas area, they are enjoying their granddaughters and retirement.

This is Ann's third book. Her first book was *Restore, Restore, Restore and More*, followed by *Restore, Restore, Restore Devotional*. Both books made the Amazon bestseller list the first week of their release.

Carlisle Hope Noble is twelve, and she is a seventh grader. Carli has won awards for essay contests, competing with all the schools in her area, and she is an amazing artist, as well.

Carli currently enjoys gymnastics, competitive cheerleading, reading, and leading children's Bible study at her school. She is always found with a book in her hand or nearby. She is a straight A student.

Carli has two younger sisters. Kendall is a fourth grader, and Caitlin a second grader. All three girls love to read and all have a talent in art. Carlisle will tell you more about herself.

More about the Coauthor

Hi, my name is Carlisle Hope Noble. I was born in 2005 in Plano, Texas, a suburb of Dallas. I have two little sisters, Kendall and Caitlin, who also contributed to this book. Kendall is nine, and Caitlin is seven. I have two Brittanies, Pepper and Coco, who are crazy, happy dogs. They make us laugh all the time.

I went to Trinity Christian Academy from first through fifth grades and loved it. Last year, I moved to a new school, Legacy Christian Academy, and am enjoying it also. I love to play soccer and am currently on a competitive cheerleading team. Everyone says I'm very crafty; I say I am a grandma at heart. I make up games for my sisters, sew, crochet, and love to cook. I'm currently trying to grow a herb garden. This month, on March 24, 2018, I found out I made the cheerleading team at Legacy Christian Academy.

Prayer to Receive Jesus Christ as Your Personal Savior

This is the most important decision you will ever make. Jesus makes it so easy to do.

"If you declare with your mouth, 'Jesus is Lord,' and believe in your heart that God raised him from the dead, you will be saved. For it is with your heart that you believe and are justified, and it is with your mouth that you profess your faith and are saved" (Romans 10:9–10 NIV).

See, our part is simple. To confess that you believe and receive, pray this prayer out loud:

"Jesus, I believe in my heart and confess with my mouth that You died on the cross for my sins, You were raised by God from the dead, and now sit next to God in heaven. I ask You to come into my life and make me a child of God. I receive you into my life as my Lord and Savior. Thank You for saving me."

"For everyone who calls on the name of the Lord will be saved" (Romans 10:13 NIV).

Yes, the very moment you committed your life to Jesus, you became brand-new, saved from death and eternal separation from God. Instantly, you were born again and have inherited eternal life with God in heaven.

God chose you, loves you, and has a wonderful plan for your life. Stay close to Him by reading the Bible and prayer, and He will direct your path.

Prayer to Receive the Filling of the Holy Spirit

Receiving the filling of the Holy Spirit is also easy. We simply have to ask:

"For everyone who asks receives; the one who seeks finds; and to the one who knocks, the door will be opened.

"Which of you fathers, if your son asks for a fish, will give him a snake instead? Or if he asks for an egg give him a scorpion? If you then, though you are evil, know how to give good gifts to your children, how much more will your Father in heaven give the Holy Spirit to those who ask him!" (Luke 11:10–13 NIV).

We know we are asking in God's will, for this is actually a specific command. Look at this verse:

"Therefore do not be foolish, but understand what the Lord's will is. Do not get drunk on wine, which leads to debauchery. Instead, be filled with the Spirit" (Ephesians 5:17–18 NIV).

Why does it say to be filled? So that we can understand what the Lord's will is. By being filled with the Holy Spirit, we will know the will of the Lord. This is not a one-time thing, but it is a continuous thing. We are to be filled by means of the Holy Spirit so we are controlled, influenced, and governed by the Holy Spirit.

It's interesting that God compares it to being drunk with wine, to be under the influence of wine.

Wine controls people, and they act in an unnatural, unsafe way under that influence. They may be hauled off to jail for harming another under that influence of alcohol, ruining their lives and possibly other innocent people.

Someone under the influence of the Holy Spirit is acting in an unnatural, but delightful, way. The fruits of the Spirit are seen in these people. They are glorifying God, blessing others, and being blessed by God in return.

Make the right choice. The Holy Spirit is supernatural, and God wants us to walk comfortably in the supernatural, as Jesus did. That is done by being filled with the Spirit, continuously controlled and under the influence of the Holy Spirit. That's not like filling a glass of water so it overflows, but it means to be continuously being led by God through the Holy Spirit, the very power of God, inside the believer.

Of course, God wants us to ask for this continuous filling of the Holy Spirit, God's supernatural power. God wants us to have all we need to live a new life.

Pray this prayer: Dear heavenly Father, I want to be under the continuous control of the Holy Spirit today and tomorrow and the days to come. I know you want that for me as well, so thank you that I have received it. Allow me to be supersensitive to the leading of Your Spirit as I am learning to walk in this fabulous way. Thank you for this wonderful gift of yours, and may You indeed be glorified through my life. In Jesus's name, Amen.

You probably don't feel different, but you do now have the supernatural power of God inside of you. As Carlisle and I discovered as we wrote the chapter about the Holy Spirit, He, Himself, wants to teach us how to be aware of Him and of His leading. Ask the Holy Spirit questions. Let Him teach.

Contact me on Ann Lynn Noble Facebook page, please, and let me know that you prayed to receive Jesus as your personal Savior or to be filled with the Holy Spirit. I would like to send you messages to encourage you in your spiritual growth.

Other Books by Ann Lynn Noble

Restore, Restore, Restore and More

Restore, Restore, Restore Devotional